All This Time in the Dark

Tessa M. Osborne

Copyright © 2020 Tessa M. Osborne

All rights reserved. No part of this book may be reproduced or used in any manner without the prior written permission of the copyright owner, except for the use of brief quotations in a book review.

ISBN: 9780578769035

Printed by IngramSpark in the USA.

www.tessamosborne.com

For my three boys. The people who keep me out of all the dark places in my mind. The three best things I've ever done with my life. You are my lights in this otherwise difficult world.

Prologue

Daisey

It has been fifteen days since I got here. Fifteen days, and all I've had to eat are Cheetos and animal crackers brought to me from the vending machine. My hair is greasy, even though I try to wash up in the shower, but I ran out of soap last week. Nobody brought me any more. I'm hungry, but the last time I asked for more food, I got slapped across the face.

They took my clothes the day I got here. I thought about asking where they went because my grandmother gave me the shirt I had been wearing. It was blue with cats on it. It was my pajama shirt. When I left home, it was nighttime. I was supposed to be in bed. I wonder what my parents thought when they woke up the next morning and didn't find their teenage daughter in her bed where she was supposed to be. My mom probably cried; my dad probably called the cops. Maybe they missed me. Or, maybe, the cops just assumed I was dead now.

When they brought me here — to the old motel off El Rancho in the middle part of town where my family never ventured — I had been excited. The guy who brought me here was already eighteen, popular, and rich, and he was interested in me. I was excited when he suggested I sneak out and meet him, so

Tessa M. Osborne

I did. But now I wish I hadn't. I wish I had stayed in my room, underneath my pink comforter, in my blue shirt with the cats on it.

It gets cold in the motel room at night. I usually sleep on one double bed and use the sheets from the other bed to wrap around my body like a toga — they're the only pajamas I have — then I layer both dirty, stained comforters over the top of me. I turn the thermostat all the way up, but it doesn't help much. The room is old, the dial on the heater crusty with age. I'm tired all the time, though I don't know whether it's because I'm cold or because I'm hungry and constantly scared.

It has been fifteen days since I was brought here, assuming I didn't lose any time. I think there were a few occasions that I blacked out. I think they give me drugs, maybe to calm me down. Once, it was because I couldn't stop screaming. Whatever they stuck in my arm clouded my brain and made it hard for me to stay awake. I try to be compliant because it scares me when I can't think for myself. It scares me when time passes, and I can't tell how long it has actually been. I hope it was only fifteen days. I hope my mom still senses that I'm alive out in the world somewhere. I hope she doesn't give up on me.

The doorknob wiggles and I hear the deadbolt on the outside click open. I'm lying on the bed in my makeshift pajamas, thinking about eating real food and watching *Nick at Nite* on TV. The shows remind me of a time far away. It's comforting on nights when it's quiet. I glance towards the door as it opens. He walks in, and I smile hopefully. I haven't seen this man since he brought me here — since I willingly got into his truck. The night he opened this motel room for the first time, me following behind, nervous but excited; he glanced into my eyes and quickly looked away. Almost like he was sorry. I want to believe he was sorry. He had squeezed my hand twice, leaned in, and whispered in my ear, "I wish I didn't have to do this." Right then, I knew something was wrong.

I tried to rip my hand from his, to turn around, but he had grasped me too tight. My stomach sank deep, and then I knew it was too late. As we walked

All This Time in the Dark

through the motel room door, I noticed someone sitting on the bed closest to the bathroom, farthest away from the door. He was a big man, kind of fat. He looked like he had a kind face. He was well dressed, all in black. Black slacks, black shirt tucked in, and a black jacket. His hair was messy on his head. The ring on his left hand sparkled with gold and diamonds.

"Hi," the big man said. He stood up and extended his hand to me. He was tall — taller than my dad — at least six-two.

"Hi," I had whispered, glancing anxiously around the room.

"What's your name?" he asked. I told him, but couldn't hide the shaking in my voice.

"I'm Mike."

"Hi," I whispered again, but my mind kept saying, *Run, run, run.* When I glanced around, the only way out was behind me, and the man who brought me here had been standing in front of the door. *When did he drop my hand?* I wondered, realizing I couldn't remember when he had walked away. He was behind me, arms folded over his chest, looking at the ground.

The door opened behind him and another man, who was also big and fully dressed in black, came in. "Are we ready yet? He's getting anxious." He gestured behind him, towards the parking lot, where an innocent blue car waited. Behind the wheel sat another man, though I couldn't make out his features.

Mike's eyes flashed angrily. "Did I say I was ready yet, man? Who the fuck do you think you are to interrupt me?"

The new man backed out slowly.

"I hear you're a virgin," Mike continued, looking into my eyes.

I hadn't responded then; I didn't have anything to say. In that situation, I remember feeling embarrassed by my virginity. I knew it was something bad, but I didn't know why it could be bad. I didn't know what I had done to make Mike look at me the way he did, or why they had brought me here.

"Lucky for you, we need more girls like you. I can get a lot for you."

Tessa M. Osborne

"A lot of what?" I asked, looking him straight in the eye.

Mike got angry then and punched me straight in the face. Nobody had ever hit me before; nobody had ever even touched me if I had asked them not to. The force of his strong arm connecting with my face knocked me back and I landed with a thud on the grayish-red motel carpet.

"Never look me in the eyes again. Do not address me. You work for me now! Do you understand me? *You* work for *me*. You do what I say, when I say it, or you will die. Do you get that? If you do what I say, you might make it home to your mommy again. If you do what I say, you will have a great life."

I cried, holding my cheek as it began to swell.

"Get up," Mike ordered.

I did as he asked.

"Take your clothes off and lay on the bed."

I cried as I stripped down to nothing, naively keeping my underwear on.

"Those, too," Mike said, gesturing toward my Hello Kitty underwear. I had worn them because they were cute, and a stupid part of my sixteen-year-old brain had hoped the man who brought me here might see them. Now that he *was* seeing them, I wished that he wasn't. I pulled them off and crawled up on the bed. The covers were cold and itchy, and I remember thinking that I didn't want to lie on the grimy motel bedspread. My mom had always said there was blood and semen on them. I had always laughed at the faces she made when she had to touch them. I cried harder thinking of her.

"Good girl," Mike said to me. He waved toward the door. "Bring him in."

The door opened and the other man in black came in, followed by the man I assumed had been waiting in the car. The man from the car looked mean and terrifying. I still don't like to think of him now.

All This Time in the Dark

"She a virgin?" he asked as he counted out bills. They looked like hundreds to me that night. I used to think that was a lot of money but, in the last fifteen days, I have seen a lot more.

"She says she is. I guess you'll tell us. Five hundred off the price if she isn't."

"I won't pay anything if she isn't."

"She's still a valuable product. I won't take less than two hundred," Mike said with authority. It made sense to me that people would listen to him. That he does what he does.

The man rolled his eyes and shook Mike's hand.

I figured out that night that my value was seven hundred dollars. It has decreased considerably over the last fifteen days.

The other men left the room, and it was just me and the man who had just paid cash for whatever he wanted with me. Virginity has a high price.

I don't remember what I did as the man came at me. I may have blacked out as a defense mechanism. A part of me wonders if that was even real. But when I opened my eyes to find myself still sitting in the dirty motel room, I remembered that it was, in fact, something that happened.

The man had tried to kiss me, but I was crying too hard. His hands started roaming my breasts first, and I felt something next to my thigh. In sex ed at school, they had mentioned that a man had to have an erection to have sex with a girl. That night was the first night I had ever seen a penis that wasn't a drawing in a book or pamphlet. One night, during a sleepover at my friend Samantha's house, we had simply googled "porn." When a bunch of websites popped up with odd videos, we had giggled loudly and quickly shut it off before her parents found out. That was the closest I had come to what was now pressed up against my bare leg.

The man didn't get undressed all the way, just pulled his pants down and lifted his shirt up a little bit. I remember thinking that was weird because, in books and on TV, the men and women were always fully naked when they made love. Maybe that was the difference between fucking and making love. Maybe that was the difference between being raped and not being raped.

I cried harder as he laid his body on top of mine. He wasn't gentle when he forced my legs apart and even less gentle as he shoved his hand inside me. It hurt, and I cried out. I hadn't had anything other than a tampon up there, *ever,* and the pain was uncomfortable. The man had whispered to me to relax a little, but I couldn't. He told me it wouldn't hurt as bad if I weren't so tense. That just made me cry harder.

It wasn't supposed to be like this, I thought over and over. After fifteen days, that thought still creeps into my head, but not nearly as loud or as nagging as it was that first night. *It was supposed to be with someone I loved. They always said it would be with someone I loved.* The harder I cried, the harder the man's penis pressed against my leg. He started moaning into my tear-streaked face and then I realized that he liked it when I cried. He probably paid extra for a virgin who cried.

When he finally pushed his penis into me, I screamed. He pulled back, startled like he didn't expect me to do anything but sob uncontrollably. For one almost comical minute, we both just laid there looking at each other — him sweating on top of me; me lying there in pain. Then his expression turned incredibly angry and he pulled back to slap me across the face. "Shut up, bitch!"

I turned away from him and saw that the blinds were still partly open. We were on the ground floor. I could see someone standing with their back to the window. Even if I tried to run, I wouldn't get very far. I tried to relax like the man had told me, but I couldn't.

He pulled his penis out and glanced down. "Huh," he said, "You really were a virgin." I didn't know at the time what that meant, but I do now: virgins bleed. The man was checking to see if I was bleeding, and I was. Fifteen days later and those bloody sheets are still crumpled in the corner of the room. I see them every time I get up to go to the bathroom.

All This Time in the Dark

"FUCK!" the man suddenly cried out before his entire weight collapsed on top of me. The pain didn't stop immediately, just dulled slightly. His penis turned slippery and he was obviously embarrassed. When he pulled it all the way out, he turned away from me on the bed, but I still saw how small he was and how much blood was on him. I didn't know then that he was small, but after fifteen days, and over thirty-two men, I know now what small is.

The man panted and cussed as he got up to find his clothes.

Before my mind went completely black, the thought crossed my mind that I would never even know the name of the man who took my virginity.

Part One

Kate

Student council was a nightmare these days. As Junior class president, I was in charge of the final dance of the school year, but I couldn't figure out what theme to use. We had all voted, unanimously, to make this final dance a Sadie Hawkins, where the girls asked the guys out (mainly because the three of us in charge — all females — didn't have boyfriends and wanted them).

I'd never had a boyfriend. I had been kissed once. A boy named Andrew had walked me home from school and, when we made it to my front door, he leaned over shakily and kissed me on the lips. I didn't know he was going to do it, but it surprised me and made me nervous. After that, every day at school, Andrew would walk me to my classes while holding my hand. I assumed that meant we were a couple and even wanted to change my Facebook page to "in a relationship." My younger sister, Haddie, told me that was stupid, so I didn't. Three weeks later, I saw Andrew walking Tammy Taylor home from school and holding her hand. I realized I didn't quite make Andrew's cut as girlfriend material.

That was sophomore year and, even though some boys had seemed interested in me, I had never been on an actual date. My friend, Jovie, had dated four different men and had sex for the first time with her boyfriend on her sixteenth birthday. She said it was magical. I was curious about anything sexual and questioned her constantly. My best friend, Samantha, was just like me. We didn't have the exciting life that Jovie did, Samantha and I just focused on school, cheerleading, and student council.

My sister was only one year younger than me — eleven months to be exact — and she dated far more than I ever did. She didn't focus as much on school as she did her social life. I desperately wanted to make my parents proud of me; Haddie would rather our parents know she was desperately liked. She was fifteen now, but for one month out of the year, we would be sixteen together. Haddie loved that. I did not. I didn't know if Haddie had had sex yet, but I knew for a fact she had gotten close. Samantha and I had listened to phone conversations through her closed bedroom door and heard her tell her friends, some of whom were cheerleaders with me.

I was nervous about planning the junior end-of-the-year dance because I knew it had to be perfect. Haddie got to come because her boyfriend was a junior, Samantha had found a boy she wanted to ask, and the entire JV cheer squad was coming. It was going to be the biggest event of the entire year, and I couldn't wait. The most important thing was finding a date for me, but I knew that could come later after the dance had been planned to perfection.

A week before the dance was scheduled, the senior football player whom everyone wanted to date, Ian, started talking to me. I had only ever talked to him when it concerned student council — he was Senior Class President — but it felt like this time was different. This time he wanted to talk to me because I was interesting, or funny, or was I maybe—*possibly*—kind of cute? I had always wondered if I were good looking. My deep black hair, bright, intense green eyes, and pale skin kind of contrasted in a way that made me *interesting*, but maybe too intense. I didn't really know how other people saw me, but Ian seemed interested, and I liked it.

All This Time in the Dark

Four days before the dance, Ian walked me home from school. My family lived in an upper class, suburban neighborhood, only a two-minute walk from the best high school in the district. My sister and I walked to and from school every day, but never together, always at separate times, or on separate sides of the street. As Ian walked with me, he grabbed my hand and, for the first time since last year with Andrew, I felt giddy.

"You seem nervous," he said, glancing sideways at me.

I laughed, "It just feels nice to hold your hand."

"I agree."

"You're walking me home, but I don't even know where you live. Is it around here?"

Ian pointed up the road. "I live on the hill behind your house."

Behind my upper-class neighborhood, there was a group of houses. Originally dubbed the Windswept Development due to their higher location, the builders had to stop construction on the rest of the development during the recession years ago. They never started building again, so on top of the hill sat seven houses — each of them gigantic, elegant, and beautiful. They overlooked the southern part of town, brilliantly sparkling in their unfinished developmental beauty.

"You live in Windswept?" I asked, surprised. I knew Ian was on the richer side — he drove a BMW and always had a new outfit on, usually Ralph Lauren, but his backpack was some ridiculous thing that Jovie had looked up once and discovered that it cost over four thousand dollars.

"I do."

"Wow!"

"Impressed?"

"More like curious. What do your parents do to afford that?"

Ian paused and turned to look at me. It seemed like he wanted to say something, like he was searching for the words. He was so handsome. His dark blue eyes and tanned skin mixed perfectly with his dimples when he smiled. I couldn't believe the most popular boy in school was talking to someone like *me*.

"My parents died when I was eleven. I live with my uncle and my brother. My brother is the one who bought the house." He looked down, almost like he felt like he had said too much.

"I'm so sorry, Ian, I had no idea about your parents. Everyone at school just thinks you're a big mystery. I think it's amazing that your brother takes such good care of you."

"They were in a car accident and neither survived. My brother was only twenty-four when they passed away."

"What does he do to afford such a gorgeous house?"

Ian stumbled over his words, confusion passing over his features. Maybe he'd never heard the question before. "He's a salesman. I'm not quite sure all of what he does. All those adult things are so boring," he said, rolling his eyes as he resumed walking.

When we got to my house, he leaned against the front gate. Haddie pushed past us like she didn't notice who we were until she saw Ian. "Ian Brooks. What a surprise." She flipped her hair in his direction and pulled her low-cut shirt down even lower. Ian said hi but didn't take his eyes off mine. Haddie got annoyed and left.

"This is where I leave you, Kate," he said.

"I guess so."

"Maybe you should call me or, at least, follow me on Instagram."

"Maybe I will."

He leaned in and kissed my cheek. He was so soft I almost didn't feel him there. As he turned to walk away, I called after him, desperate for our interaction to keep going. I had butterflies in my stomach, and my heart was beating so fast, "Ian! Wait! Would you want to go to the Sadie Hawkins dance with me? I know it's just a stupid junior dance, and you have prom coming up, but it could be kind of fun?" I felt heat creeping up my neckline.

All This Time in the Dark

"Sure! That would be great!" He smiled with his dimples. And I was in love.

Daisey

They call me Daisey now. Mike decided the night after I lost my virginity that my face was "worthy of a daisy." He said it while he caressed my face and stuffed his hands between my legs like I was his pet. I hate the name Daisey. I hate being called that. I hate the way the men look at me when they call me Daisey.

The door opens and the man who brought me here comes in. He tries to look at me and, even though I smile a little, I don't want to see his face. I notice he has someone behind him. At first, I assume it is another man, but then I see a sweet face and realize it's a woman. I haven't been with a woman since I was brought here and, until now, I always assumed the only people who abused women were men. I never thought a woman would pay for me. He pushes her into the room and walks out.

The girl next to me is tiny. She is shivering and her hair is greasy like mine. It doesn't look like she has tried to wash it, though. She stinks.

"Hi," I say to her.

She glances toward me without saying anything. She looks at me the way I look at the men who come through the door here. Even wrapped in my toga, I wonder if she thinks I paid for her. *Does she know where she is?* I wonder. *Does she care?*

"They call me Daisey. They said I couldn't use my name anymore or else I would tell you what that was." I tried to mouth it to her. I think they are listening. They are always listening. I always see a shadow just outside the door, either sitting or standing. I know they can hear what I am saying. On the rare occasion I catch a glimpse outside, I can tell we are on the bottom floor of the motel, and our door opens to the parking lot. Behind that is a hill and trees, and sometimes I can hear the sounds of a freeway. I assume we are on the far back side of the motel. I never see any other cars in the parking lot. Sometimes, I am afraid that one of the men who took me owns the place.

The tiny girl finally looks up at me. Her face is worn and her skin weathered like she has been outside for a long time. I wonder if she is homeless; I hope she isn't, but it looks like she probably is.

"They said to call me Angel. That's my name now. I've had a lot of names, though — call me whatever you want."

I nod, "Angel is nice."

"One of the nicer ones, I guess."

"How did you get here?"

She looks at me, confused, like I should know because I got here the same way. "I asked them for a job?" It comes out as a question.

"I don't understand. You *asked* to come here?"

Angel turns to look me. "How old are you?"

"I'll be sixteen in a few weeks."

"Why did *you* come here?"

"They tricked me. I thought one of the guys out there was my boyfriend, but he brought me here instead."

"Oh."

I back up and sit down on the bed closest to the bathroom, the one I lost my virginity in. Despite that, I have found some comfort in this bed the past few weeks, mainly because I know the right way to smush around and get comfortable and warm in the night. Angel still has her clothes on; I wonder if she'll share something so we can both stay warm.

"I sleep here, usually. You can sleep in the other bed, but we need more blankets."

She looks around the room. "The last place I lived was the street, so at least I have a bed."

"You were homeless?"

"Not by choice. My mom kicked me out when I was thirteen. She liked drugs too much and she couldn't afford me and crack at the same time."

"How old are you?"

"Seventeen."

Her answer startles me. She looks so much older. Her face has deep lines in it and her hands are worn like leather. In the dim light of the motel room, I had thought she was incredibly dirty, but now I start wondering if the dots that line her arms are something else. I'd never been around or known anyone who had tried drugs before. Some of the kids in school talked about smoking weed on the weekends, but I had always been too scared to try it.

She sees me looking at her arms. "Track marks, kid. I wish I didn't have a thing for drugs and needles, but I do. I guess Mama gave me something after all."

I nod and lie back down. The sun is starting to set and once it's all the way dark, my nights usually get busy. I'm sore. Everything aches. The thought of anything else going inside me today makes my stomach turn. It feels like my crotch is on fire. It hurts when I pee, and pain shoots through me every time I am forced to have sex with another man.

"Have you had sex before?" I ask Angel. I assume she has, given the worn-out look on her face.

"I had sex for the first time when I was nine. My mom needed drugs and she could get a lot of money for me back then."

All This Time in the Dark

I want to throw up. The way she says it is so matter of fact. "Ouch," is all I can manage.

Angel laughs, "Yeah, ouch."

I laugh, too. She has kind eyes and a sweet smile. She was probably a really cute kid.

"I'm sorry that happened to you."

"Me, too. But Mike promised I would live a better life here. I need a better life."

"You met Mike?"

"He found me sleeping on the street the other day. Told me if I worked for him, I would have a better chance of surviving. It's better than being raped, robbed, and starved."

"They don't feed us much. Chips."

Angel laughs, "I haven't eaten in two days. If someone wants to buy chips for me, I'll take it."

I stand there looking at her, each of us in separate worlds, but somehow united in this one. It doesn't make sense to me, but I'm happy for the company, relieved that I don't have to be alone with my thoughts anymore. I hope she won't have to leave.

The door opens and Mike walks in, followed by a man I haven't met before. They look back and forth between the beds.

"Get up," Mike orders. I stand immediately; Angel takes more time.

The man behind Mike has two big shopping bags. I hope there is food inside. I'm so hungry it hurts.

"Here. Clean yourselves up then put these on, we're leaving in an hour."

They dump the bags on the bed and leave. We each take a bag and dig through it. Cheap soap, shampoo, makeup, and perfume are on top. Beneath the perfume, that smells like flowers, are tall high heels that come to a steep point. Mine are black and Angel has red. I pull out a dress that doesn't even cover my butt all the way and the neckline is cut all the way down to my belly button. Angel has a pair of red shorts and a red bra to wear. Both outfits look like they have been worn before. They smell that way, too.

Angel walks into the bathroom, so I assume she is taking a shower first. I sit down on the bed and sift through the makeup. I can't remember the last time I caked makeup all over my face. I generally didn't wear much when I was in school — it took too long to put on in the mornings.

It feels nice to have a real shower with actual soap. I finally feel somewhat like myself, except for the ache in my crotch and the unrelenting pain in my gut that tells me what is about to happen isn't something I want to happen.

After we stuff ourselves into the clothes that are two sizes too small, Mike and the other man, whose name I do not know, load us into the back of a black SUV with tinted windows. I used to think only famous people drove around in cars like this, but I guess I was wrong. In so many ways, I was wrong.

Mike turns around and faces me in the back seat. He lays his hand on my thigh and runs it up my leg, his thumb grazing the crotch of my panties. I don't like the feeling. I don't know why people say they actually like sex. I never, ever, want a man to touch me ever again. I turn to look out the window as we drive, but I don't recognize any part of this side of town. I didn't grow up here. I have been driven an hour outside of where I live, and this is completely new territory for me.

We turn to get on the freeway and my stomach drops. I am moving farther away from home, and never going back to that motel room again. I feel so deeply depressed. I want to cry or scream or try to get out of the moving car. I thought that, as long as I was in that motel room, there was still a chance someone could find me. My friends had known who I was going to meet the night I snuck out of my house. They had known, and they would tell the police when I didn't come home. They would tell who I had been with and where we might have been going. Even if it took the police awhile, I had assumed they

All This Time in the Dark

would look everywhere they could within at least a one-hundred-mile radius. That's how it worked on TV — why didn't it work that way in real life?

Why weren't the police kicking down the door of the motel or suddenly chasing the black SUV with their lights flashing and sirens blaring? Why wasn't some strong woman detective with ugly shoes putting a random blanket around my shoulders and taking me to a hospital where McDreamy and a team of doctors were waiting to clean and feed and comfort me? I had been sure — *so sure* — that my chance of being found at that motel, any day now, was so wonderfully high.

As we drive away from the motel — and any small measure of comfort I have known — I sink down in the seat and close my eyes. I don't know where we are going, and I don't want to know. I don't want to do anything but die.

11

Kate

Ian came to pick me up for the Sadie Hawkins dance and I was glowing. I had spent the night before combing the mall with Samantha and Jovie, hoping to find the perfect dress. I found a beautiful golden one and a purple one I really liked, but the white one with sequins was the winner. The sequins glistened and the white strapless dress fanned out long behind me as I walked. It was like a wedding dress, but even more beautiful.

Jovie spent the entire day on Saturday at my house. We did our nails, curled and hair sprayed every strand of hair on our heads until nothing moved. Our faces were covered in every kind of sparkly makeup we could find. I was glowing and the excitement I felt was tangible, like someone could just reach out and feel me buzzing.

I had never had a boyfriend before. I hoped this meant Ian was turning out to be one. I hoped it meant he liked me, and we were going to start dating for real. I hoped this meant he would kiss me — *really* kiss me. I wanted a real kiss so badly, especially a kiss with tongue. I had seen people French kiss before, but I'd never known what that felt like, and I was desperate for Ian's tongue in my mouth. For anybody's tongue, really.

All This Time in the Dark

When Ian showed up at my house, he told me I was stunning. He shook my father's hand. He hugged my mother and kissed Haddie on the cheek. She blushed as she walked away and, for the first time, we traded a giddy look that said we were both just stupid girls who couldn't believe this god of a boy was in our own home. Ian took my hand and slipped a corsage onto my wrist; I pinned one to his coat. It was like prom, our Junior dance, but it was so much more. It was the best night of my life.

As Ian escorted me out the door to his waiting car, he placed a hand on the small of my back. I felt a weird tingling sensation rush through my body. I wasn't sure where it came from or what it meant, but everything about me felt amazing. I felt more alive than I ever had. I didn't realize boys could be so exciting; life was so much more than plans and grades, cheerleading, and student council. I didn't realize how much I was missing and why Jovie said she liked sex so much. But I was starting to understand why my parents always found a way to touch each other or a secret way to make sure the other one knew they loved them. I wanted that feeling, too. As we walked into the dance, I wanted the chance to hold Ian's hand while everyone watched, so the whole school knew that he was *mine*. That we were *together*. That he was my *boyfriend*.

We danced the entire night and, as a sad Taylor Swift song ran rampant over the sound system, Ian pulled me up to his chest and danced with me so close that I could feel his heart beating. As the song wore on, he sweetly put one finger under my chin, tilting my head up to meet his.

"Hi," he said as our eyes met.

"Hi," I mouthed back.

"This night has been wonderful."

"I know. I'm so happy you came with me."

"I always think the girls are just after me for my looks or for my money, but I never thought a nice, smart girl like you would be interested in me."

"Of course, I'm interested in you."

"You're beautiful, too, I forgot to say that before. You make me nervous."

"*I* make *you* nervous? *How?*"

"You're just gorgeous. And you're so smart and everybody in the school likes you. People just want to use me. They genuinely *like* you."

"They just know I can help them with their homework."

"I don't think so," Ian laughed. "You're more than you think you are." Then he leaned down and kissed me long and slow. He pulled back, smiled, and leaned forward, his lips brushing against mine timidly before pressing in harder. I didn't notice his tongue was anywhere near my mouth until the kiss was over, and then I realized we had been making out in the middle of the school dance. Everybody saw us together. That meant more than just walking down the hall holding hands.

I giggled, sounding way more stupid than I actually was, "You're so good at that."

"You're better," he said, pressing his forehead to mine.

"I don't have much practice."

"It doesn't matter," he said back, and then kissed me again.

***

Ian walked me back to my door three minutes before my eleven-thirty curfew. He was a true gentleman. My parents already loved him; I could tell as soon as we'd left the house earlier. Any hesitation they had about letting their sixteen-year-old daughter date an eighteen-year-old man had dissipated the moment they met him.

"I'd invite you in, but my parents are probably asleep."

"Nah, I should go anyways. My brother worries if I'm home too late. We're all each other has in the world anymore." I noticed he always looked down when he talked about his brother.

All This Time in the Dark

"I thought you had your uncle, too?"

"I do, but we're not close anymore. He just helps out on the nights my brother works late."

I nodded and smiled, "Well, goodnight then."

"Wait!" Ian grabbed my waist and pulled me into him. My hand rested on his chest; his eyes burned into mine. "I can't let my girlfriend go home without one final goodnight kiss."

"Your girlfriend?" My heart was beating so fast, I felt it might beat out of my chest. "I'm your girlfriend now?"

"Only if you want to be."

"I do."

"Good, it's settled then. Go change your Facebook status," he said with a wink. He kissed me one more time, hugged me close, and walked off towards his car.

Daisey

It is morning by the time I open my eyes again. I am in a different motel room now, this one slightly nicer. It is still a motel, and I am still on the ground floor. When I open my eyes, I see the curtains have been thrown open and a there is a palm tree outside. We don't have palm trees in Reno. Either we have crossed the state line into Arizona or California, or we have traveled down to Las Vegas. When I was six, my parents took me there, and I lost my first tooth in the pool outside of the hotel. There were palm trees everywhere and I had been mesmerized by their tall, scratchy trunks.

I rub my eyes and notice that my arm is sore. There is redness on my bicep, and, upon closer inspection, I find a small puncture wound. I had been drugged. They had drugged me in the car after I fell asleep in the back seat. *Where's Angel?* I thought. *Did they drug her, too?* I look around, hoping to see the woman I was brought here with, but I am alone again. The last motel room was dark and drab; this one is white everywhere. At least the sink doesn't have a crack in it.

I push off the bed, still in my black dress from the day before. I'm not wearing any panties, even though I had been wearing the black lace ones they gave me. I notice a bloodstain on the white bedspread where I had been sleeping, almost a perfect circle seeping beneath the covers. *What the fuck?*

As I try to stand up, I realize the lower half of my body is in too much pain to move. I scoot to the edge of the bed and crumple to the floor before crawling my way towards the bathroom. I sit down on the toilet, frantically wiping every part of me I can to see where the blood is coming from. It isn't my period like I was hoping. It is coming from my ass, and every time I touch my butt, it hurts even more. The blood is pouring from me and, for a second, I want to scream out for help. But I know I can't. I try to see what is happening in the mirror, but it is too hard to look at that area without a handheld mirror.

"FUCK!" I scream. I don't know why I do it, or what I hope to achieve, but everything hurts so damn bad. "FUCK ALL OF THIS!"

I fall to the floor in tears. I don't understand what is happening to me. I am dizzy and disoriented, and everything beneath my waist hurts like I've been split open. My inner thighs are purple, and I can see the marks where someone's fingers had dug into my skin and left bruises. My ankles are bleeding, raw, and red. There are perfect circles of red around them like I had been tied up. Or, maybe, tied down.

Mike opens the door, I think perhaps in an effort to calm my shouting, but he just tosses Angel in and then slams the door shut behind him again.

"Angel!" I yell out of sheer relief.

She looks panicked when she sees me, "Holy shit, what did they do to you?"

"I don't know, can you help me? I'm bleeding!"

"I know, your face…"

"No, my ass. What do you mean my face?"

"Honey, get up and look in the mirror."

I do as she says and see a cut from my forehead down to the left side of my cheek. The headache suddenly makes sense.

"I don't know what happened, but I can't walk."

Tessa M. Osborne

Angel slowly picks me up from the floor and helps me back to the toilet. "I know you probably don't want me to look, but I have to make sure this bleeding is stopping. Is it okay if I look at you?"

I shrug, "Sure."

It doesn't take long before her eyes bore into mine. "Have you ever had anal sex before?"

"Huh?"

"You know, ass sex. Sex up the butt."

"Is that a thing?"

"Well, yeah."

"People have butt sex with girls? I thought that's where men had sex with each other." I don't want to sound stupid or immature, but I just don't know these things.

"Honey, people do anything they want to girls."

"What about it? The ass sex?"

"That's what happened. Someone forced their dick inside your ass and ripped your asshole a lot. It might need stitches."

"I don't have stitches. I don't even have a phone to call for help. They took the phone out of the room like they did the last time."

Angel goes to the front door and bangs on it as loudly as she can. A man pokes his head in, another one I have never seen before. "What the fuck is going on? Keep it down in there!"

"She's hurt. One of your girls is hurt. Her value goes down if she's hurt — you and I both know that. You have to help her."

A thought flashes in my head that, if they take me in for stitches, I can tell the nurse or doctor who I really am, and then they can save me. There has to be an Amber Alert out for me. I am a minor and was supposed to be at home in my own bed the night I went missing.

The man glances at me like he is bored and then sees me lying on the floor. "Did you do that to her?" he asks Angel.

All This Time in the Dark

"What the fuck, man, no!"

"Hold on."

He comes back ten minutes later with Mike in tow. Mike's eyes widen slightly. "Who did this to you, Daisey?" he asks me.

"I don't know."

"What do you mean you don't know?"

"I think someone drugged me."

"I drugged you to get you out of the car and into the motel," he said, like I was stupid and should have known that all along.

"I don't remember what happened last night."

"We got here three nights ago."

Shit, shit, shit, I haven't remembered anything for three days! I don't even know where I am anymore! "I can't remember anything from the last three days."

"Shit!" Mike shouts and punches at the dingy hotel wall.

The other man bends toward Mike's ear and says, "Sir, we thought she was the one you were talking about."

"How much did you give her? We can't take her to the hospital!" Mike yells. I've never heard him yell like that, like he is ready to kill someone. He seems panicked.

Angel is standing off to the side. "They put me in a different room for two nights. She was in here alone with a john. They took me out when they brought him in."

"The guy paid for two nights. We didn't make him leave. But we came in every so often and made sure she was okay," the tall man whispers again in Mike's ear.

"And drugged her more," Mike answers.

The man refuses to look away from the ground. "I don't know."

"You were supposed to drug *me*," Angel says, "I was the one you promised the drugs to as payment for what I did! Now *she* has them, and I have

19

none, and I'm going crazy here! You have to help me, Mike! I need something, anything! I can't stop shaking!" Angel looks panicked. She runs to the bathroom to throw up.

"Fucking disgusting whore," Mike says as she runs off. He looks at me. "We need to clean you up, but we can't take you to a hospital, do you understand?"

I nod weakly without looking in his eyes.

"Lay down, someone will be here in a minute."

"Angel," I mutter.

"I'm here, honey." Her breath smells rancid, but she grabs my hand and, even though I pretend her hand is my mothers, I grasp on for dear life and never want to let go.

Kate

I spent the entire week after the dance floating between ecstatic and madly in love. I didn't care that I barely knew Ian, only that the most popular boy in school was now calling me his girlfriend. Everyone was jealous, including Jovie, and Jovie was never jealous of anybody.

"Did you guys have sex yet?" Jovie asked as we walked to English class together.

"Jovie! I'm not that kind of person. You know that."

"Well, at some point, everybody has sex. Think about it. Your old grandmother had sex and that's how you got here. My next-door neighbor, who has a lot of birds, probably had sex one day, too. You have to do it."

"I don't have to do it *now.*"

"No, but you don't want to wait. I heard the older you get, the worse it hurts when you finally do have sex."

"Sex hurts?"

"It hurts when they pop your cherry for the first time."

"What's that?"

"I don't really know, but when they pop your cherry, you bleed, and it feels kind of weird. It hurt for me, but the second time doesn't hurt as bad."

"Why would it hurt more when you got older?"

Jovie laughed, "Jared told me that when you get older, your cherry, whatever that is, gets tougher, so it's harder to pop it."

"Jared told you that?" Jared was Jovie's nineteen-year-old boyfriend. The best friend of her brother, Jared, seemed to know everything about everything.

"Yeah, before we had sex. He told me it wouldn't hurt that bad because I was younger."

"Oh, I didn't know that." I hoped Jovie and Jared knew what they were talking about because I wanted to have sex with Ian. I knew it sounded insane because we had only been together for a week, but I just loved him so much. I didn't know sex was supposed to hurt, though. All anyone had ever told me, including my mother, was that sex was something between two people who loved each other. I knew the logistics of what was supposed to happen — a man put his parts in my parts — but after that, I had no clue.

"Do you think Ian will be able to tell I'm a virgin?" I finally asked Jovie.

"Of course, he will. You'll bleed, like I said, and you won't know what you're doing."

"I have to know what to do?"

"Well, I mean, the actual sex part you'll have to know what to do a little bit. Not as much as the guy, though."

"Like what?" It had never occurred to me that, after the man put his parts in my parts, something else would actually have to happen. Like, didn't we just lie there? In movies, they always just laid under the covers panting, and then made a lot of noise before they came out from under the covers talking about how amazing it was.

Jovie laughed, "Just have fun with Ian!"

All This Time in the Dark

"I'm nervous."

"Don't be. Sex is fun, and having a boyfriend is even more fun." Then she flipped her hair out behind her and ran off to English class.

Daisey

After a few hours, a woman I don't know comes in and uses super glue on my ass. She says the glue will hold it together. The bleeding has stopped, but I still feel confused about where I am and what is happening. Angel tells me that they'd given me the drugs meant for her, that every time the john stepped out to make a phone call, one of Mike's men came in and shot me up again. That's how Angel puts it, but she never says what they shot me up with.

Apparently, only certain drugs can be injected, and not all of them are usually used like that. Still, all I had ever really heard about was weed. There was a rumor that some guy at school had gotten in trouble for snorting cocaine in P.E. class, but nobody ever talked to him to find out if that was true.

"You could have died, honey," Angel says to me. Our motel room is finally quiet as all the men have left us alone for a while. While I look worse by the day, Angel seems to be thriving in the new environment she chose. Maybe it is the regular access to drugs and a shower.

"You look better," I say to her, as if that is an answer. I don't really have any answers anymore.

All This Time in the Dark

"I feel better than when Mike found me. I had a john yesterday that scared me, though. He wanted to tie me up, and Mike said he wasn't allowed to tie up his girls, but as soon as the guys left, he did it anyway. He held a knife to my throat the entire time he fucked me. I thought I was going to die." Angel starts laughing and I wonder how she could ever actually think that was funny. She just casually mentions the time she got raped at knifepoint and thought it was a good thing she didn't actually die. I wish I were dead. I wish someone would come and stab me, so I don't have to live out the end of this story.

Eventually, I won't be worth it to the men who have me. Eventually, my price will fall so low that I won't be worth the stress and hassle to keep me. Eventually, they will kill me or let a john kill me, and being killed by a man who has also fucked you for money seems like the worst fate imaginable.

"What happens when they're done with you?"

"The johns? They clean themselves up and leave."

"No, Mike and his guys. What happens when they don't want me anymore?"

Angel rolls over on her bed and props herself up on one arm. "I would guess they probably trade you or sell you."

"Sell me? They're already selling me."

"No, I mean, sell *you*. Not sex with you. I've heard guys like Mike make most of their money by trading their girls or selling them to men in other countries. Mike is pretty well known on the streets, especially with young girls like me. He gives us a chance — he's willing to help us. He has a good reputation out there."

I should be scared by what is to come, but nothing scares me anymore. Nothing makes me startle or jump. After we left the old motel room, I just assumed I was going to die at some point. My body is bruised and beaten and broken. I feel like I am a hundred years old.

"Why would you want to work for him if you know that, one day, you'll be sold to someone else? That sounds terrible, Angel."

"Mike said he wouldn't sell me. He said when I got too old to turn tricks, he would let me help him with the business side of things. The way I see it, I'll always have a place to sleep at night, he feeds me, and there's a steady supply of Dynamite. I can't complain."

I had never asked what her drug of choice was. The track marks were all I needed to see. Whatever they had injected me with was something I didn't need to know about. But I make a mental note that, if I ever get out of this situation and make it back to a computer, I am going to google what the fuck Dynamite is and why she keeps talking about it the way she does. Because when they give it to me, I always just feel out of control and close to dying.

"I hope you get the life you want," I finally reply, unsure what would be the right thing say.

Three days later, or at least I hope is three days, one john comes into the room. Usually, when a john comes in for one of us, the other goes to the bathroom for privacy. We don't have to do this, but we respect each other enough. Plus, I don't want to watch Angel get fucked. Occasionally, a john will come in and demand the other girl leave — they're almost always married, almost always afraid that the greasy, half-dead girl in the next bed will somehow tell their wife about what they're doing.

But as the man approaches my bed and Angel gets up to leave, one of Mike's guys comes in and pushes her back down on the bed. "What the fuck, man?" Angel says.

"He wants both of you," Mike's guy answers and backs out of the room.

Angel and I glance at each other. This has never happened before. I don't know what it means, but I don't know how to deal with a threesome. My ass still hurts.

The john tells us to both lie down on my bed together and spread our legs apart. We do as we were told because, if we don't, Angel will lose her home, and I will get beaten again. We roll over in submission because, as young

All This Time in the Dark

women, men decide what we do with our bodies and, if we fight, they will win. Men always win. Always.

Angel is shaking next to me, and I assume it is because she needs more drugs in her system. She isn't usually afraid of what the johns have her do, because there is a good chance she has already done it before. He licks us both, one after the other, and keeps commenting on how we "taste." I hate it when men say that about me. I know I probably don't have any kind of flavor except disgusting, given my hygienic state and the fact that I had already had sex with two other men today.

"Fuck each other," the man says as he steps back. His flabby, fat penis is hanging out of his pants like it is waiting for something to do.

Angel and I look at each other. We know we have to do it, but I don't know how. I don't know if Angel knows how either, but I figure she does. It seems to me like there isn't much Angel doesn't know.

Angel rolls over toward me and whispers in my ear, "Relax, honey, it will be over soon, I can tell."

Kate

Ian and I had spent every day together for the last two weeks, and my parents were mad.

You spend too much time together, they had said. *We're worried about your schoolwork,* they whined. They obviously didn't understand how love worked. They just didn't get it. I told Ian I loved him, but he only smiled and kissed me when I said it. His eyes looked sad. I wondered if he was thinking about his parents, I wondered if he wanted me to meet them. I wanted him to say it back to me, but I didn't ask him to. I tried to focus on school and student council, but the only place I wanted to be was cheer practice or with Ian. At least at cheer, they understood why I was so in love — all the girls were jealous of me and asked me about him constantly. It felt nice to be worthy.

"We're worried you're spending too much time together, Kate. He's so much older than you," my mother said one night.

"He's two years older than me."

"He has a car. He's a senior. He'll be in college next year."

"He's going to college here in town."

All This Time in the Dark

"It doesn't matter," my parents consistently badgered. "It's not good for you to be so obsessed with him."

I knew they didn't understand. Halfway through high school and I had never lied to my parents. I had never been to an actual party before, just slumber parties with the girls. Ian was my first real kiss. I had stopped counting Andrew as a kiss, mainly because he didn't matter anymore. Nobody mattered except Ian.

"Fine," I lied, "I'll go to Samantha's after school tomorrow instead of seeing Ian. We'll study together. Does that make you happy?"

Haddie was sitting in the corner of the living room, painting her nails. She looked up upon hearing me and mouthed at me from across the room, *Are you lying?* I held her gaze for as long as I could and didn't say anything. She knew. My parents knew, I could tell they knew, but they seemed relieved at my answer, relieved that maybe there was a chance I was finally listening to them.

"That's all we want, Kate, just to know you see past this guy. That there is more to life than just a guy."

"But you two met each other in college. I'm only two years away from college now. What does it matter if I find a guy two years before the age when you guys met?"

"You just have so much growing up to do still."

"I'm more grown up than you think."

***

Later that night, Haddie came into my room. She perched on my bed as I was texting with Ian, telling him about the conversation with my parents earlier in the day. He agreed with me and, over text message for the very first time, said he loved me and was afraid my parents would come between us. I texted Samantha a screenshot of it right away. Even though she was wary that he'd said it for the first time through text, she didn't say anything negative to me.

"You aren't going to Samantha's after school tomorrow, are you?" Haddie asked, interrupting my thoughts.

"No, but you can't tell Mom. Please don't tell Mom."

"I don't know if you should see Ian anymore," my sister said. She looked concerned. She took life so seriously.

"Not you, too, Sis."

"No, not because of that bullshit about love. I don't buy it and neither do you. You can be in love at any age. But I've heard some things about Ian from some of the girls lately. They said at a party a few weekends back, he got drunk and screwed a girl in his car in the front yard. She's saying she said she didn't want to have sex with him. She's saying he raped her."

"Who was it?"

"Taylor O'Donnell."

"Taylor likes drama; she's probably making it up."

Haddie looked serious. Her eyebrows furrowed under her bangs and, for a second, she didn't look like the teenaged adult she tried to be. She just looked like the little freckle-faced girl who used to steal my Barbies and eat all the marshmallows out of the Lucky Charms. Her bright green eyes looked serious, and as she talked, her black hair brushed her shoulders. "I don't think you know Ian as well as you think you do. Taylor is saying she was raped. By Ian."

I paused. I wanted to take her seriously, but Taylor was notorious around school for picking fights and causing drama. Why would Ian rape somebody anyways? He he'd never done anything more than kiss me — he hadn't even tried. "I don't believe it, Had. I think she's making it up."

Haddie got up then and left the bed. "Please be careful, Kate. I think Taylor is telling the truth."

"Close the door behind you," I said, as Haddie walked away.

Daisey

I finally saw my Amber Alert on the television last night. I was watching the local news station, mainly because the shit hotel didn't get any TV stations except 2, 4, 8, and sometimes another cable channel that I couldn't quite make out, but it sounded like they spoke Spanish or Russian. The news broadcaster didn't say anything about me, but there was a black ribbon running along the bottom of the screen. It said my name and then in bold letters:

Missing. White girl. Black hair. Green Eyes. Last seen on June 8th, 2019. Parents miss her very much. Reward being offered if found.

It said I had been missing for twenty-eight days. Almost a full month, and there were at least three days I couldn't keep track of, three days that I had no recollection of. My picture flashed on the TV screen and Angel said, "Holy shit, that's you!"

"I guess so."

"Your parents want you back."

"And?"

"Can't you ask Mike to send you back?"

"It doesn't work that way, Angel. I didn't come here because I wanted to. The only way my mom will ever see me again is at my own funeral."

"I always thought you lied so you sounded better."

"What?"

"Like the story of how you got here. I thought you got here the same way all the girls do because we have nowhere else to go."

"I don't think it always works that way. Some of us are sold, even though we don't want to be."

"I'm not."

"You're a fool."

Angel looked sad, like her best friend had said she hated her. "No, I'm not," she answered quietly.

"Yes, you are. If you think you'll ever be able to leave here, then you're a fool. They won't let you leave alive, Angel."

"I can leave whenever I want, I have that choice."

"No, you don't. Try to walk out that door right now, and you'll be beaten within an inch of your life. Or, better yet, try to *ask* Mike to let you leave. He won't do it. You're his property now. And even if you could leave, where would you go? You're the perfect target. You have nobody looking for you, and you need Mike to help you. If you didn't have him, you'd have to get sober and find a job. A *real* job, one where you got paid in something other than dope or needles."

Angel started crying. "I can leave whenever I want!" she sobbed, getting out of her bed. The clothes we had were all that was available, so when she ran towards the door, her boobs bounced out of the skimpy purple bra, and her ass hung out of her purple satin shorts. "LET ME OUT! LET ME OUT! LET ME OUT!" she started screaming as she hit the door over and over again.

32

All This Time in the Dark

I sat up on my bed, but didn't move towards her. If the door opened, I didn't want to be the one they caught. I didn't want them to think I had done this.

The door swung open, and one of Mike's guys stomped in, "What the fuck is going on here?"

"I want to go! I want to go home!"

The man laughed, "This is your home now, bitch."

"Mike said I could leave whenever I wanted!"

"Guess what, whore, Mike lied."

"I want out. I don't want to do this anymore," she pleaded. Whether she was trying to prove a point to me or trying to show the man she could get out, I don't know, but I hoped she would stop before she got hurt. I had ruined the vision of the life she thought was saving her. I had taken that dream from her and killed it. She always said she would get out; it shouldn't have mattered to me if she did or not. But I was so angry. I was angry with myself for being in this situation, I was angry with Mike for putting me in this situation. I was angry with Angel for putting *herself* in this situation. I didn't know who to be the maddest at, or where to put that anger, so I caused Angel to hate herself. *You did this,* I kept thinking over and over.

"We. Don't. Give. A. Fuck," Mike's guy answered. He talked so slow and got right down in Angel's face when he said it.

Angel spit in his face. I watched it run down his forehead into his eye.

"You bitch!" the man yelled. He walked towards her; I ran to the bathroom and shut and locked the door.

I heard him shove Angel against the wall, heard her body slam into the floor. "You think you can do whatever you want?" the man growled, as he either kicked her or hit her over and over again. I heard her grunt and cry out, but not much after that. "Who the FUCK DO YOU THINK YOU ARE?" he yelled again.

Tessa M. Osborne

I heard the table in the corner by the window hit the floor, and I didn't know if it had fallen on her, or if she had been thrown at it. I hoped maybe it was an accident. After that, the only sound I heard was that of the man repeatedly stomping on the ground. He was a big man, and every man who worked for Mike wore big, thick, steel-toed boots. I hoped the boots were stomping on the floor and not on Angel. I wondered why nobody else in the motel stepped in, asked what was wrong. Then I realized: these men, these men in power, could do whatever they wanted. Men who think women are better seen, not heard, are used to getting their way. They're used to beating on people smaller than them or people they feel are weaker than them just because they can. Because, at some point in their lives, someone had made those actions permissible, and the feeling of power was too much for them to lose.

"Gary, what the fuck?" I heard another voice say. It was another man, though not one I recognized. It wasn't Mike's. I hadn't seen Mike in days. As far as I was concerned, Mike owned me, these men, and maybe hundreds of other women like me. He had more to worry about than two little girls who barely brought in $1,000 a week, even though we fucked three men a day.

"This bitch tried to escape! I was sitting outside by the door, and she tried to open the door and leave. When I stopped her, she attacked me. I didn't have a choice."

"It happens, man. Mike will get it."

"You think?" the man, who I guess was named Gary, said.

"It's happened to all of us a time or two. Mike doesn't care, he'll get another. Where's the other girl, though? Weren't there two in this room? There's only one in the room upstairs."

"She ran into the bathroom. Hasn't come out."

"Fuck. Fine. Whatever. We can't do anything about it now. We have more to worry about. Leave her here and Strobe will come in and clean this up."

I heard the men leave, the door slamming closed behind them.

All This Time in the Dark

I opened the bathroom door and peeked around the corner. I didn't know what was left out there — it didn't sound like much — but I hoped the only mess "Strobe" needed to clean up was the room.

Instead, I saw Angel lying on the floor. Her shorts were torn, hair flung over her face, one arm above her head. Purple bloomed across her stomach. A dark purple bruise bloomed around her belly, blending in with the purple of her shorts. It was mesmerizing in a way that I suppose only death could be.

"Angel?" I said softly, brushing the hair away from her face.

But Angel didn't have a face anymore. I replayed the stomping in my head — the sickening thud of the boot slamming into the floor — and then I realized it wasn't the floor the boot had been hitting. I couldn't see her eyes anymore, or her nose, her forehead blended in towards the floor.

"Angel?" I said again, thinking maybe she could answer. Thinking maybe she was still in there... somewhere.

"Angel, wake up," I said, shaking her arm. It bounced unnaturally — not like a regular arm, one that was intact, one that wasn't broken. But it wasn't her arm anymore. Nothing about Angel was Angel. Not anymore.

I sat back on my heels and cried. I cried harder than I had the night they took me. I cried for Angel, seventeen-year-old Angel, who didn't even have a real name. She had told me once she liked the name Amber. That, one day, she was going to change her name. I told her it was pretty, that I liked Amber, too. I cried for the woman she wanted to be, and the life she thought she would get the chance to live.

I held her hand and noticed that the scars from the drug needles weren't just on her arms — there were puncture marks between her fingers, too. I cried even harder.

Growing up, everyone told me *drugs are bad, bad people do drugs*, but there I was, holding the hand of a girl who hadn't had a choice. She wasn't bad. She had the purest heart of anyone I had ever known and, for her, drugs were the only escape she had from a world that had left her behind.

Tessa M. Osborne

Angel had sex for the first time when she was nine years old. She never knew what safety felt like, never knew what it felt like to be held in the arms of a mother who loved her. She couldn't remember a time when she wasn't scared, or alone, or hungry, or just plain exhausted. Nobody had stopped to help her over the years because *drugs were bad, and she was bad for doing them.* Nobody thought she was worthy of a kind word because all they could see were the bad choices she made. "Like I can choose anymore," she had said to me.

I thought about my mother. When I was five, I went through a phase where I couldn't sleep at night. I kept waking up with these horrible nightmares. One night, maybe out of pure exhaustion, my mother let me cuddle up in her bed, where I felt so safe. She held me against her, cradling me in her arms. She kissed the back of my head, and I fell asleep, tucked tightly against her, knowing nobody would ever be able to hurt me as long as she was there. Angel never had that. Girls like Angel never knew what that was like. When she was nine, and that man was hurting her, did she ever close her eyes and hope her mom would come save her?

Was *I* supposed to save her? Could I have stopped Gary?

I had been too scared to leave the bathroom. I had been too angry to try and stop Angel from getting so upset. I had wanted to hurt someone, and Angel was the only person in the room. I didn't want her to die for what I had said. I didn't want any of this to happen.

I ran to the bathroom and threw up. There wasn't much in my stomach, but I threw up over and over and over again until I was just heaving over a toilet that hadn't been cleaned in weeks. I leaned back on the cold, tile floor and rested my head against the wall. I didn't know if I believed in God, but I was here, and Angel was gone. Somewhere out there, my mother was probably looking for me, and Angel's mother wouldn't even notice if she wasn't there anymore. I hadn't even known that this kind of evil existed in the world.

All This Time in the Dark

"Please, God, if you're there. Please help me. Please get me home. Please let Angel just wake up. Please don't leave me alone in this room without her. Please don't leave me here."

I cried until I fell asleep on the floor.

Kate

The local news was playing in the background during dinner. It dinged three times as a warning that something exciting was about to happen. My mom glanced toward the TV.

"It's an Amber Alert," she said. Every time we heard or saw one of these, she would hug my sister and me, like it could have been about us. It always seemed like something stupid for her to do. Where would we go?

"It's just another teenaged girl. Probably ran away to do drugs with her boyfriend," my father said from the kitchen.

My mom hit him on the shoulder as she walked by, "Robert!"

"Well, it probably is."

"What if it was one of our girls?"

"Our girls would never be on the TV like that because they know better. We raised them better."

I looked at Haddie and rolled my eyes; she smiled back at me.

Mom came over and hugged us. "So many teenage girls that have gone missing the past few months. I read a news article that said they were worried it was a sex trafficking ring somewhere close by. They had that one bust in Sacramento earlier in the year."

"There's no sex trafficking happening here, Jessica. We live in a nice neighborhood, and the girls go to a good school. Nothing will happen here. That kind of stuff happens on fourth street, where people live in motels and don't have any money."

Haddie glanced up from the table and looked towards my dad, "That kind of stuff can happen to anyone, Dad."

"I should see if that family needs help," my mom said. But we all knew she never would. She wasn't that kind of person. She didn't help people like that, because deep down, she believed like my father did: that girls made poor choices and got themselves into their own mess.

"Dinner was delicious, thank you," my father said.

"You're welcome, dear," my mom answered, and she got up and started clearing the table.

***

The situation with Ian and Taylor seemed more serious now. People were talking about it at school. Most people assumed Ian was right and telling the truth. But Samantha had stopped talking to me because she believed Taylor. She said women had to stick together. Maybe she was right.

When I asked Ian what happened with Taylor, he didn't want to talk about it at first. He tried everything he could to avoid the question. I kept asking and he finally told me they'd had sex in his car two months ago, outside of a party. He said she wanted it, too. I didn't like hearing that Ian had already had sex with other girls, but he was eighteen and I couldn't assume the most popular boy in school was still a virgin.

"How many other girls have you had sex with?" I asked one night while we talked on the phone. I should have been asleep hours ago. I had a history test in the morning. The last History test I took I failed. My mom still didn't know but, when she found out, she would say it was because of Ian.

"I don't want to answer that, Kate."

"Please, I need to know."

"Why?"

"Just because I do."

"I had sex with Taylor, but that wasn't the first time we had been together. We had sex three times before that. That's why I don't know why she cares about the time at the party. Before Taylor, I had sex with two other girls."

"Who were they?"

"What, like you want their names?"

"I guess."

"You wouldn't know them."

"Oh."

"They graduated last year."

"Okay, then," I said and changed the subject.

Daisey

I had a break from entertaining the johns while Mike's men decided what to do with Angel and, consequently, me. They didn't know if they should move me to a different room, so I could still make money, before she was cleaned up. Mike was out of town, and with him gone nobody seemed to know which way to go. We were stuck in an endless loop of hell while Angel's body rotted on the floor.

Instead, they kept me trapped in a room with a dead girl for three full days until Mike came back into town. I hadn't known what "out of town" meant or where he would go when he got there but, when he finally came back, they decided it was best to let Strobe take care of Angel and to move me again. I barely acknowledged them as they entered the room, mostly because, once Angel died, I lost the will to try to live. If they could kill her so easily, I knew they wouldn't stop themselves from killing me. They knew it would be easy to replace us when we were gone. We were dispensable to them.

We hadn't been established with Mike long enough to have regular johns. He was just trying to find out how to fit us into his world; he was trying to see where we belonged in his long line of women. Occasionally, when I was lying in bed at night and the men outside thought I was asleep, I could hear them talking to each other. I knew there were more girls upstairs above me. Sometimes I could hear them having sex. Other times I just heard Mike's men talk about the ones "up there."

It didn't sound like this was where Mike preferred to work, and Mike's men kept hoping there would be a day when they could join all the men "up there." Wherever that was. I wondered if that meant there were more of us out there somewhere. I hoped it meant I wouldn't have to be alone for too much longer. I longed for the days when Angel was there to keep me company. Angel and I had talked about everything together. She knew me better than anyone ever had before. I told her about school, my parents, my boyfriend — or the man I thought he was. She knew how I got here, what I wanted to believe was going to happen to me. At night, when it was dark and quiet, I would tell her that I hoped I was dead.

"You don't want that, Honey, trust me. I've been around death enough. When you're dead, that's it, there's nothing left of you."

"My parents would miss me, I think."

"Nobody would miss me," she always said.

I wondered if she knew I was missing her. I had promised myself that if I made it out of this, I would tell the whole world that she had existed.

A few nights before Angel died, we were lying in bed talking about the first times we'd had sex. The first time, for each of us, we had been sold for a price. The first time, for each of us, we had been raped. We talked about how bad it hurt. Angel told me she had never had an orgasm, that she had never felt anything from a man other than disgust. I didn't doubt it since her whole life could be summed up by the events of my last month.

"After the first guy raped me, I bled for two days on the motel sheets. I didn't know what else to do."

Angel had laughed, "That's normal."

All This Time in the Dark

Anytime I worried about anything, Angel made me feel like I didn't need to worry at all. She had seen and done everything and knew that time healed. She knew that the next day something worse might happen, so what was the point of dwelling on the pain? I loved that about her.

***

Strobe was on his way to move Angel. They stuck a needle in my arm and shoved me into the back of a black SUV. They always drugged me when I had to go outside — probably so I wouldn't fight them, but they didn't know I would never fight them anyways. I didn't see the point. Angel died from just saying the wrong thing. If I ran and got caught, I wouldn't make it out of that. I knew that and so did they.

I didn't want to end up on TV as the girl who *was*; I only wanted to be the girl who *is*. Whoever I was. Daisey, now, I guess.

Mike was in the front seat. His men always said he spent too much time worrying about me. Maybe because I was so young, or because he knew people were looking for me. When Angel disappeared into Mike's circle of evil, nobody even blinked. She walked off the street, holding his hand, and nobody said a word or tried to stop her. Nobody tried to get her back. People were trying to get me home.

"How's my beautiful Daisey doing today?" Mike asked. He placed his hand on my thigh, always up high. Always too high.

I nodded as an answer. He asked me questions, but never wanted to hear the response.

"Sorry you had to see Angel like that, love. It was a shitty experience for all of us."

I nodded again.

"We're going to move you to the main house." He seemed excited by this announcement and watched me expectantly, like I should be excited, too. Like he had just said he was buying me a puppy.

I nodded and half smiled, so he would think I was happy. I didn't want him to think his announcement went unheard. I was afraid. I was always so afraid.

"I think you're ready for me to take the risk and move you in."

I stared at him, but my eyes landed on his nose. *Don't look in his eyes. Don't look him in the eye.*

"The owner of the motels we've been staying at don't mind trading for them to keep their mouths shut and give us the run of the place, but those are for our temporary girls. The ones like Angel, who we don't think will last long. They give us free rooms; we give them free pussy. You know the drill."

I didn't know all of what he meant. It sounded like a crock of shit to me. Angel would have lasted longer than me if she were still alive — maybe he meant the drugs would have taken her. I also didn't like how he'd said "trading" with the motel owners. *Trading sex for them to mind their own business.* I didn't like the way it sounded.

I stared at Mike's mouth.

"I don't like drugs in the main house. We keep that separate."

I glanced down at my arm, where they had poked me with the needle. I could feel the drugs, whatever they had given me, clouding my brain. I tried to fight it, to stay awake, to hear what Mike had to say, but I couldn't do it. My eyelids were so heavy.

He must have seen me look down at my arm. "It's just a small tranquilizer, not drugs," he said, but by then, I was too tired to even care.

Daisey

I opened my eyes. The room I was in was small. It looked like someone had taken a regular room and cut it in half. To my right, there were bars running across a window; to my left was a door. In front of me was a small dresser with nothing on top of it. There was a nightstand next to me with a small TV that looked like it was made in the 1970s. I glanced down at myself, hoping I was alone and that I wasn't naked.

I was completely alone, dressed in a long black nightgown — the satin kind my mother usually wore at night when I was a little girl. My feet were cold. There was a white comforter on the foot of the bed, and I thought about covering up and going back to sleep, but I had to know where I was first.

I tried to look out the window, but couldn't see much through the bars. All I could make out was the top of a few trees, so I knew I wasn't on the bottom floor anymore. I couldn't see anything else.

I tried the door and, much to my shock, it opened. *Try to run. Maybe you don't have to be Daisey anymore.* I peeked into the hallway; it was long and dark, with doors running along each side. All of them were closed. If I was in Mike's main house, there were more girls behind those doors. I counted five, plus mine at the end. The hallway ended in a bathroom and then curved away, and I couldn't see any more.

The house smelled musty, too many bodies shoved in a too-small space for far too long. Kind of like when someone rolls out of bed and brushes their teeth, but they still smell like stale sleep.

I took a step into the hallway, wondering if there could be traps here. I wouldn't put it past these men to try and trick me. Sometimes I wondered if they were looking for a reason to kill me. It was too risky for them to keep me alive now — now that they knew someone was looking for me.

I tiptoed down the hallway, hoping to see someone. Another woman like me would have been great, but I wasn't holding my breath. As I approached, I noticed that the last door before the bathroom was ajar. I leaned in hoping to hear movement, but there was nothing. I pushed it open another crack, just so I could see inside. Just so I could see what was in there.

"You shouldn't do that," a voice behind me said.

I jumped, yelping, and flipped around.

"Sorry! I didn't mean to scare you! You're new; I was just trying to help."

"I'm sorry," I replied, although I didn't know quite what I was apologizing for.

The woman in front of me was thin and blonde. She looked better cared for than Angel had been. She was wearing a nightgown, like me, and no shoes. I always liked shoes and socks. I missed my socks.

"Don't be sorry, sweetie. That's Sugar's room. She's occupied right now."

"It was just so quiet in there."

The woman shrugged. "Some of them are quiet, I guess."

"I'm..." I paused. I almost said my real name, out of sheer habit. "They call me Daisey."

All This Time in the Dark

"That's a new one. I guess Mike is starting to run out of food names. I'm Honey."

I teared up slightly, and I didn't catch myself fast enough to prevent a tear from rolling down my cheek. "A friend used to call me honey," I said back.

Honey wiped the tear from my cheek. "You'll have friends here who will look out for you. Our hallway is pretty open unless we're working, which a lot of us are a lot of the time. But you must know that by now. None of us came here first. How long were you in the motel for?"

Honey knew where I had been; she had been there, too. It was a relief that someone else knew what I had come from. "Around a month, I guess."

"That's the longest stay yet! What did you do for that honor?"

"I don't know. People are still looking for me, they moved me to two different motels."

"They looked for me for a long time. I've been here for two years, though, I don't know if they'd be looking for me anymore. I used to see my name and face on TV. It always gave me hope. I don't think I have much hope left anymore. Or, rather, this is just kind of home now. I guess, anyways."

"Is it terrible here?"

"Not as bad as the motels, really. I promise. The johns that come here are all higher scale. They pay good money for us girls since we're in a clean and safe environment. And we've all been screened for diseases. Mike knows what he's doing."

"I haven't been screened."

Honey laughed, "Yeah, you have, you were just knocked out and didn't know it. You don't know how you got in here, do you? They do that so you don't know where you are, so you couldn't run even if you tried."

"What do they give us?"

"Some girls say we're close to overdosing when they do that, but I don't know."

"It scares me."

"I'm scared all the time," Honey said back.

"Do we get to eat here?"

"We get breakfast, lunch, and dinner, as long as we're quiet and do what we're told. Mike is here a lot; he makes sure we're well taken care of. We're his property — he wants good money, he needs to take good care of his product. But, truthfully, we still don't get that much to eat. Lunch is usually like a sleeve of Ritz Crackers. Dinner last night was spaghetti, but we only got one bowl. It could be worse, I guess."

"How did you get here?" I asked her.

She glanced around, maybe so nobody would hear her answer, "Come to my room."

"Is that allowed?"

"I guess not, but nobody ever stops us. We can't be together if a john comes in. The rules are simple: don't leave the hallway. You go to your room and the bathroom. You can go into another girl's room, but only if they're alone and only if they invite you in. Don't leave the hallway. Do you understand? They don't think twice before they hurt you. But you look like you already know that." She turned and started walking toward another closed door.

"Do I look that bad?"

"You look like you took one hell of a beating," she tossed over her shoulder.

"Everything hurts, all the time."

"They screen the men better here, trust me. You're pretty safe from the johns, just not from Mike or his men."

"Mike's Men," I said, laughing.

Honey laughed, too. "Exactly. So, welcome to my room. It's right next to yours." Honey's room looked just like mine, but her comforter was black instead of white. It was empty — so empty. And the walls were dirty — stained — like so many people had come through here without it ever being cleaned.

All This Time in the Dark

She tucked her feet underneath her and sat on the bed. I waited awkwardly in the doorway. "Oh, girl, just walk in. It's not like it's a private space."

"Thanks."

"So, you asked how I came here? Well, that's a complicated story, I guess, but the easy answer is that two years ago, I was on vacation in California with my parents. I went for a walk on the beach one night with these guys I didn't know. They seemed so nice and funny. We had a few drinks — illegally, I suppose, since I was underage. Anyways, I wanted to show my parents that I was seventeen and knew what I was doing, but as we walked further down the beach, the men started acting weirder and weirder. Someone must have walked up behind me because I remember being stabbed in the neck with something and I woke up at a shitty, hole-in-the-wall motel. And I've been with Mike ever since. Two years. It's been a long time."

The thought made me want to die. "I'm sorry."

"Me, too," Honey answered, "but I could be dead right now, so I guess I have something to be thankful for."

"Sometimes, I wish I were dead. It would be better than getting fucked in the ass again."

"You a virgin?"

"I guess I'm not anymore."

"There's a difference, you know, between having sex with someone you actually like and being raped. 'Cause that's what this is. This is rape. Don't ever let anyone tell you differently. Rape is rape is rape is rape. There is no way around that."

"I always thought I'd lose my virginity to my boyfriend," I said, starting to cry. My black eye hurt when tears hit it; it must have cut open again. My eyes never seemed to heal from always being hit.

"You will. One day when we make it out of here. It will be so different, I promise."

"I hope you're right."

Tessa M. Osborne

We stared at each other for a long time before Honey's door burst open. She glanced at me and rolled her eyes. "I guess it's time to get to work now," she said.

Kate

Some of my friends didn't think it was a cool thing to walk down the hall holding Ian's hand anymore. But I was still in love with him, so why did they matter anyway? All that mattered was Ian and me. Me and Ian. When my parents caught wind of the little problem with Taylor, they refused to let me see him again. They said he was "dangerous."

"Act like an adult, Kate," they said.

"Think about how much you're worth," my mom cried. What did that even *mean*? I knew my grades were slipping a little and that my student council activities had fallen mainly on the vice president, but I was in love for the first time in my life, and now my parents were acting like Ian was a villain when, *clearly*, he was not! It just wasn't fair. They thought they knew my life better than I did. Who knew what was better for me than *me*? It just wasn't right!

The school year came to a close, and summer crept in. I spent the first few days enjoying the warmth in my backyard. My parents said I couldn't see Ian, but they couldn't stop me from having him over to swim in our pool when they were gone at work all day. We only had security cameras in the front yard,

51

and I knew where their dead spots were. I could sneak Ian around back and my parents would never know.

We made out in the pool every day, but never more than that. Ian never touched me; he never even tried. I wanted to go further — I had decided I was ready to lose my virginity — but Ian made it clear that he was scared to even go near another girl after what had happened with Taylor.

"Taylor doesn't matter to me," I said one day as we were kissing by the pool.

"It matters to my reputation," he said, "I can't have sex with other girls when Taylor is still coming after me. Think of my family."

"But you're eighteen now, so your family can't do anything anyways."

"I can't shame them like that, Kate."

"Nobody would have to know. I wouldn't tell anyone."

"Please don't pressure me, Kate." He always ended up saying this. Like a woman could ever pressure a man. I didn't even think that was possible. All men wanted to have sex all the time. Wasn't I every teenage boy's dream?

One day, a few weeks into summer, I got tired of just kissing and tired of waiting for Ian to make a move. "I can't do this anymore!" I wailed.

Ian looked startled. "What? Do what?"

"I can't keep just kissing you, Ian! I can't do it! I need more. Don't you care how badly I need more from you? I love you, Ian!"

Ian pushed me away from him and started to walk towards the front gate to leave, "I can't have this conversation again, Kate."

"IAN! PLEASE!" I begged, mainly so he wouldn't leave.

"I can't do this! I don't WANT to have sex with you, Kate! Don't you get that? I don't want to have sex with you!"

I started to cry and claw at his shirt, "PLEASE don't leave, Ian! Please! I won't ask you again!"

"I think we should break up, Kate. This has gone too far," he said, as he reached for the handle to open his car door.

All This Time in the Dark

"Ian, NO! PLEASE!" I cried. "Please don't leave!"

"I can't have this conversation again; this has gone too far. It's too much. I love you, Kate, that's the problem. Don't you see that? I actually love you now and I don't want to hurt you. I have to go."

"But Ian!" I shouted after him.

He slammed the door in my face and started the car. I hit the side of the car, and then kicked it, before Haddie ran outside, "Kate! Kate, stop it!" she shouted as she grabbed me around the shoulders.

"He broke up with me!" I yelled in Haddie's face. He still hadn't driven off, and I wasn't sure why. He was just sitting there watching us.

"Kate, stop being so dramatic," Haddie said back. She was inches from my face, her hands tightly gripping my shoulders.

"He *can't* just break up with me, Haddie, he can't!"

"He can, and he did."

"No! Ian, wait, PLEASE!" I turned back to Ian's car. He avoided my gaze, put the car in gear, and drove away.

I sobbed in the front yard. I was sure my parents could see us on the cameras, but I didn't care. Ian was gone, and I was alone forever. The man I loved was never coming back. *How could he do this to me?* I thought over and over.

Haddie hugged me, but her eyes were wide like she didn't quite understand what she was watching. "Kate, he's just a high school boyfriend."

"But we were in love, Haddie! You don't just leave the people you love!"

"Some people do, Kate," Haddie said, and turned around to walk back inside.

Part Two

Daisey

I've been with Mike and his men for over a year now. I think my eighteenth birthday came and went sometime in the last few weeks, but I've lost track of so much, including if I might or might not be pregnant.

    I'm not allowed to leave my room unless I have to go to the bathroom. When the men are all downstairs, the girls move around and mingle in the hallway. As long as we're not too loud, Mike's men don't really seem to mind. All the windows upstairs are barred anyways; we can't go anywhere. And just sitting in my room gets so boring. But we have to work. We always have to work. Except when we're on our periods — then things are different.

    There's a huge calendar on the wall in the bathroom. It's on a dry erase board, so we can change it if we need to. The johns who come in aren't allowed in our bathroom, so I guess Mike figures it's okay to hang the board in there. I asked the girls a few times, and they always just shrug and say it has always been there, and they don't know any different. They always seem tired when they talk; we're all always tired.

    Mike makes us put our names on the calendar on the day we start our period and end it. He says this is for scheduling purposes only. It surprised me, but some johns prefer women when they're bleeding like that —.it makes me cringe every time I think about it — but the majority of them hate it so, during that time, we go from three to five men in a day to just one or two. The other girls call it their vacation week.

As I sat on the toilet, relishing the relative quiet for a few minutes, my eyes wandered to the calendar. I realized I hadn't had to chart my name on its white spaces in too long to remember. Everyone else had their names on the board except me and one other girl — and she was pregnant.

From what I had heard, she was only a few weeks away from giving birth. I had only talked to her once. She hardly ever left her room. At night I could hear her crying through the walls. I didn't know anything about being pregnant, but my mother had always told me the first sign of pregnancy was a missed period. I couldn't remember the last one I had. Everything here just seemed to blend together. I was malnourished, constantly stressed, and overwhelmingly anxious all the time. Maybe that was the problem.

I didn't know who I could talk to about this. In that moment, sitting there on the toilet, I felt so little and ineffectual. I missed my mother so much. I missed my friends. I missed having any woman in my life who would know better than me. In that moment, I was so angry I was stuck in this situation. I was so angry that I had been forced into a life I didn't want and didn't have a choice in. Nothing that happened to my body was own choice. And, if I were pregnant, whatever happened to me or to the baby wouldn't be up to me either. And that's the problem, isn't it? That women, like me, like anyone, aren't allowed to choose what happens to them. Our bodies are up for debate and discussion, our misery and pain subject to what some old white man sitting in an office somewhere deems acceptable or not.

I hadn't felt like myself in months. I didn't know what that even felt like anymore. I didn't remember how to laugh or smile or play. I couldn't remember the sound of my favorite song or the smell of rain. I hadn't been outside in three months, not even for a walk. I didn't remember what it was like to run or jump. I couldn't remember the feel of soft carpet between my toes or grass under my feet. I didn't remember the taste of mac 'n' cheese or what biting into a piece of pizza felt like. There were so many things from my old life that I took for granted that I couldn't even remember now. I was living life as a slave and fucking for money that I would never even see. It wasn't *my* money, but it was my body.

I got up off the toilet, angrier than when I had sat down. I peeked out the door before I left the bathroom, hoping none of Mike's men were wandering the hall. They were under strict orders never to fuck us, but sometimes they snuck up and did it anyways. We all figured out a long time ago that if we fucked them, they wouldn't say anything when we came out of our rooms and would sneak us extra food with dinner. Most of us came here by being taken; a few chose this life and realized too late that there was no way out. We were all starving. We were all just trying to survive.

Honey's door was cracked open, so I figured she wasn't working. We had to shut our doors all the way, or the johns would complain. Most of the johns were married — they didn't want anyone to know they were there. Like we could say anything. Like we could tell anyone. Like we even had access to the internet or a telephone.

"Come in," Honey said, probably thinking I was her next job. She was lying on her bed in a white nightgown. We were all given long nightgowns, sheer or satin, to wear day in and day out. It was better than the toga I made out of sheets, but it would have been nice to have underwear. I missed my underwear so much sometimes.

"Can I talk to you?"

Honey smiled, "Always."

"I don't remember the last time I wrote my name on the whiteboard," I said.

For a few minutes, she looked like she didn't get it. *She's wondering what whiteboard,* I thought. Her smile disappeared after a while, and her eyes grew panicked, "What the fuck?"

"I don't even remember the last time I had one."

"Are you sure?"

"I think so," I said.

"Did you tell anyone?"

"Just you," I said, starting to cry. "I don't know what I'm supposed to do." Crying hurt my constantly bruised face. If one of Mike's men weren't hitting me, one of the johns was always grabbing me too hard. They weren't supposed to hit me, but they could choke me, or push me, or throw me, and I couldn't remember the last time I wasn't bruised in one way or another.

"Don't say anything to anyone yet."

"I don't even know if it's true. What if it's just stress?"

"Would that matter?"

"I don't know. You're supposed to know, you're older."

"By two years. I was only sixteen when I came here. I know about as much as you do."

"Should I talk to Candy?" I asked, wondering if the pregnant woman across the hall who nobody ever talked to would have the answer.

"I guess you can try, but she doesn't talk to anyone that much."

"I don't know what else to do."

"Whatever you do, don't say anything to Mike," Honey warned.

***

Later in the day, when I was done working, I knocked on Candy's door. Nobody knew each other's real names. I knew hers wasn't Candy in real life, and she knew I wasn't Daisey, but that was the extent of it. We didn't dare mumble our real names. *Maybe you just are Daisey now,* I often thought. *Maybe that is your real name.* Those thoughts tortured me as I slept at night.

All This Time in the Dark

"What?" Candy said.

"Can I come in?"

"Who is it?"

"Daisey."

"Oh, I guess," she said. She didn't get off her bed as I came in. She looked huge, her belly sticking straight up in the air. She was wearing her nightgown still, but it was stretched tight over her stomach, like she could barely get it on. "What's up, Daisey?"

"I need help," I said, sounding small.

She looked at me like she didn't quite understand. She never talked to us, and we never sought out her help. One of the other girls said she had been there the longest out of anybody, but I didn't know how true that was. Here at the house, we all felt like veterans at this life now. Her face fell as she realized the only reason I would even talk to her, "Fuck, Daisey, are you pregnant?"

"Maybe," I said. My voice shook as I said it. I felt like throwing up. My hands were vibrating at my sides. My heart was beating so fast. "I don't know."

"I haven't seen your name on the board," she finally said, like she just understood.

"It hasn't been up there in too long."

"That's a problem."

"I know."

"Don't tell Mike."

"That's what Honey said, too."

"It's smart advice."

"What do I do?" I finally asked her. I didn't know what her answer would be. I didn't know if I wanted to know.

"There's nothing you can do. Do you understand? There's absolutely nothing you can do. It isn't your baby. It isn't your body. You should know that by now."

"You're about to give birth," I said stupidly, staring at her huge belly like it could explode at any minute.

She sat up and stared right into my eyes, "It doesn't fucking matter. It still won't be my baby. As soon as the baby is born, which will happen in this grungy, disgusting room, probably on this very bed, Mike or one of his men will take it away. They'll leave it outside a fire station, most likely. They've done it before. Or, worst-case scenario, the baby will stay here with me and be groomed from a young age to do what I do. To do what you do. If it's a boy, he'll have a better shot of getting out this shit hole. But you and I both know boys can still be sold. And if you didn't know that yet, I suggest you get your head out of your ass."

I just stood there. I couldn't find the words. I wanted to run away, but I also needed to know what else she had to say. I needed to find the answers somewhere, even though there were none.

"The thing is," she continued, "I got pregnant eight months ago. I can trace it back to a week or two when it could have happened, but in that time span, I fucked twenty-three different men. There are twenty-three men who could be the father of this child. I've been pregnant here three times before, but I had a miscarriage each time, and I've never been more fucking grateful for anything ever in my life. Because bringing a child into this world is the worst pain imaginable. I'm only twenty years old. I've been with Mike for three years, the longest of anyone in this hallway. I hate it, Daisey. I hate my fucking life.

"And what's worse, I loved my life before. But I went missing three years ago and nobody came to look for me. Or, if they did, they never found me. We're too hidden here. This is where it ends for us, Daisey. For girls like you and me. We didn't want to end up this way. I was an honor student. I had just gotten into Stanford and was about to go away for school. I was *happy*. But I made one wrong, stupid, fucked up mistake: I got into a man's car with a friend, and neither of us knew him. We were idiots, and we thought it would be okay. 'People accept rides all the time,' we laughed. 'It could never happen to us,' we said. And we got in, just because he offered, and it sounded like fun. And we never went home again.

"You know what's even more fucked up, Daisey? My friend fucking died. She died. They shot her in front of me because she tried to run. As soon as the car stopped, she started to run, and they shot her. So, I just sat there and did what they said because I thought, if I could just stay alive, it would all be okay. But I was so wrong. It's not okay. It will never be okay. I wish they had shot me that day. I pray every day for them to just shoot me and let me out of this hell."

By the time Candy was done talking, I was crying. She was stone-faced like she felt nothing. She absently rubbed her belly, and I just sat there dumbfounded. *If* I was pregnant, I couldn't be as strong as she was. If I was pregnant, I would find a way to die. I had to. I couldn't do this anymore. I couldn't do this forever.

"How did you know?" I finally asked.

"What? That I was pregnant? Or that I would never go home?"

"I don't know. Both, I guess."

"I didn't know I was pregnant for a long time. That, or I just didn't want to believe it. But I remembered my last period, writing it on that fucking whiteboard. And then one day, I couldn't remember the last time I'd needed to write it down. It's so fucking invasive, isn't it? That whiteboard. Like men have a right to know what is happening with my own body."

"I wish I could know for sure."

"You'll know one day. You'll feel nauseous doing something and realize that it's not normal. Or the smell of certain foods will suddenly be stronger. You know what it was for me? The cum. From the men. It never occurred to me that it smelled like cleaning products until I was pregnant. Like Ajax. It just has that underlying bitter smell to it. It's a heightened sense of smell I guess." She shrugged like everything she had said was no big deal.

"But when did you realize you were never going home? Don't you miss your family?"

Tessa M. Osborne

She looked mad then, "Of course, I miss my family. Don't ever talk about my family. I miss my mom and my sister. I miss my big house and my comfortable bed. I miss the way my mom's cooking smelled. Sometimes, when I'm just lying here, I try to remember what that food tastes like, and I can't, and I get so mad. I get so mad, Daisey. It has been three years and I can't remember what bacon tastes like. I want to be at home so badly it hurts. It actually aches deep in my stomach, like someone stabbed me. I'm just a child, you know? I'm just a kid. I was taken when I was so young, and sometimes I get so mad that I have so much life left to live, and yet here I am. A half-dressed whore, in a dirty bed, with filthy sheets, that three different men have laid on today."

"I wish this wasn't happening to you. Or that I could fix it." I said, my voice sounded pathetically small, even to me.

"Daisey, don't you get it? There's nothing we can do. If we try to run, they'll kill us. If we try to stand up for ourselves and demand more food besides the goddamn crackers, they'll beat us. Or starve us. Both are bad, but the food is worse. If we don't say or do anything, they'll walk man after man in here to fuck us. And then we have to just lay in bed like a goddamn blow-up doll. There is no fix here. There is no winning. This is it for us. This is how our lives end. And when we're too old to be sold here, they'll sell us to the men they work with in other countries. If we're too old for *them*, they kill us. Stop being a child. You're never going to fix this. You're never going to make it home."

The tears were pouring down my face as I stood up. Even though Candy was right, she was too bitter for me. I still had too much hope to believe in what she was saying. I still believed in good too deeply — that hadn't been fucked out of me yet. But maybe it would be. Maybe we would all end up like Candy one day. I was starting to realize that life wasn't as amazing as I had always thought it would be. I knew, now, that I was privileged with the way I grew up. I hadn't faced anything I couldn't handle. But I couldn't handle this.

I walked back to my room, realizing my stomach was growling. All I had eaten in three days was the box of Ritz crackers they had given me. The

All This Time in the Dark

box was supposed to be my lunch for the entire week. We didn't get dinner last night. None of us really knew why, but one of the girls said they heard Mike's men talking and saying we were running low on money. Mike hadn't been to the house in a few weeks and time seemed frozen when he was gone. Nobody knew what to do, except what was expected of us. If we ran out of food, the men didn't care. I had one roll of crackers left and I was so hungry. I wanted to eat the whole thing. I was already thin when I was taken, but now my hip bones poked out from underneath my nightgown and, when I laid down on my side, my inner thighs didn't touch each other.

  I thought about what Candy had said, how this was it for us. Maybe her friend had it right the night they were taken. She tried to run and had been killed. Shot dead. Maybe it was a painful way to die, but to me it didn't sound that way. It sounded better than being a slave for the rest of my life, and then deemed too worthless to even be sold. Dying sounded better than this.

Kate

My father eats a lot of meat, drinks beer or alcohol, and then he stinks. I'm convinced that anyone who eats stinky meat like sausages and drinks alcohol afterward will always smell. The smell makes it impossible to want to sit next to him on the couch, so on the nights when he's stinky, I go to my room and make up an excuse not to be with the rest of the family.

I would prefer to be on my own. I like being alone with my thoughts. I like laying on top of my bed and listening to music. I used to sneak off to my room during these nights and just text Ian for hours. But I don't do that anymore. I hadn't talked to Ian in over ten days. After he left my house, he never called me again. He never returned any of my texts or Instagram messages. He had just disappeared. I missed him so much. I missed the man I loved, but nobody seemed to understand.

Everyone in my life just kept saying I was "better off," like that made any sort of difference. That didn't help when I felt like dying from a broken heart. That was just condescending. Because they were saying the man I loved was an idiot and I was stupid for falling for him in the first place. I still loved Ian — that hadn't changed. I still hoped, every time my phone rang, that it

All This Time in the Dark

would be him on the other end of the line. I hoped he would text me again and just say, "I'm sorry," and everything would be okay.

I was sick of waiting. I finally made a decision. *Cover for me,* I texted to Haddie. She and I had become closer lately. Maybe she finally felt like she knew me, but I think most of it was that I finally understood *her.*

Where are you going? She texted back. She hadn't been driven away by my dad's smell yet, but she usually didn't last much longer than I did.

I have to see Ian.

That's a terrible idea.

Please cover for me.

Fine.

I heard her get up from the couch. "I'm exhausted. I think I'm going to get some sleep early."

"Is everything okay?" my mom asked. The tall ceilings downstairs echoed and reflected the conversations. Haddie and I had figured that out when we were little and would lay in our room, side by side, without moving or making any sound. If we laid perfectly still, we could hear my parents' conversations when they thought we were asleep. That was how we found out the Easter Bunny wasn't real. That was how we found out that our grandpa cheated on our grandma. That was how Haddie and I found out our Aunt Darcy was actually homeless and a drug addict and not in India without service like my dad had always said.

"Everything is fine, Mother," Haddie answered, "but Kate texted me that she was going to go to bed because she's tired, and I think I'm exhausted, too. We both just had a long day in the sun."

"Okay, Honey, sleep well. Kate must already be out since she didn't come back downstairs."

I pictured Haddie shrugging. She always shrugged when she thought someone was being stupid. She was usually too kind to just tell them they were dumb. Above all, Haddie had a good heart. She loved fiercely.

Tessa M. Osborne

I heard Haddie pad down the hallway toward our rooms. We used to share a room with pink ballet slippers on the walls. Now, we each had our own room with a shared bathroom in between. My parents had a bedroom downstairs. I used to be scared of the dark and too afraid to walk all the way downstairs alone in the middle of the night. I would run to Haddie's bed and curl up next to her. She was always so little and tiny. I would wake up early in the morning and run back to my bed and fall back asleep, so Haddie never knew I was in her room. The last thing I ever wanted was for my little sister to know that I was scared of something she wasn't.

She knocked lightly on my door. "I'm going with you," she said.

"You can't do that," I answered.

"I sure as hell can. You shouldn't be going alone."

"I'm older than you," I said, like it mattered, but I didn't have much to go on.

"I'm smarter."

We looked at each other, but our minds were already made up.

That was the first night we decided to leave.

Daisey

The worst part about being a whore is the sex. I used to think that was the only part about being whore, but it turns out it isn't. It turns out there's more to it than that. I'm also someone men want to dress up like a doll in clothes they bring with them. I'm also someone men just want blow jobs from, although I quickly learned that those were almost as bad as sex because they're so fucking boring. Some men want to beat me up, and I have to let them. One time a man snorted cocaine off of me — or I assume it was cocaine — and then had sex with me. I didn't like that one so much.

The sex doesn't hurt unless the man is particularly rough — it's more like I just don't feel anything at all. Most of the time, I end up just staring at the ceiling, or the floor, or the bed, and I make a bet with myself about how long the guy will last. Then I start counting the seconds until he's done. The farthest I've ever counted to was thirty-five hundred. I know it seems like a lot of counting, but there isn't anything else to do or think about. So, I just lay there and count. Or stand there and count. Sometimes I sit and count, but that's rare. I've learned that these kinds of men almost always want control.

Surprisingly, there have also been a few women, but I don't really count them. They always act like they feel guilty about coming to the house, like they know they're doing something wrong. They all look at me like I'm dirty (which I am) and act like I smell (which I'm sure I do).

It has been three days since I talked to Candy and nobody has seen her since. She has been locked in her room. Sometimes we can hear her crying, but usually, it's just quiet in there unless she has a john with her. We can always hear the customers in our hallway. The men get loud most of the time. They're just loud creatures in general, I guess.

I was on my second client of the day when we heard screaming coming from Candy's room. The john fucking me from behind, immediately dropped his hands from my hips, and froze. I felt him go soft and fall out of me and, when I turned towards him, he looked embarrassed. If the guy wasn't satisfied when he left my room, I almost always got hit. Mike's new favorite pastime was whipping us with belts. Usually, just once was enough to get the point across, but if Mike knew that this guy left without finishing, I was probably in for more.

"I'm sorry," I said, like the screaming was my fault.

"What was that?" the guy asked. I never knew their names. Most of them used fake names.

"Another girl, I guess. But we don't need to focus on that, baby, unless you like other girls with us?" I playfully tickled his neck like an idiot. I didn't know how to turn a man on, given that most of the men who had sex with me were turned on just by the thought of being able to do whatever they wanted with me.

The man seemed kind as he gently pushed me away from him. He pulled his pants up and grabbed his wedding ring off the table next to the door of my room. He slid it back on his finger. *Shit,* I thought, *Mike is going to hate this.*

All This Time in the Dark

We heard another scream, this one louder. Something fell off the wall in the hallway and crashed to the floor. Once upon a time someone had hung stupid pictures of flowers in the hallway and I guessed they were probably gone now.

"What the fuck was that?" the guy asked me like I wasn't sitting in the room with him knowing everything he knew.

"I... I... I guess I don't really know." I dropped my attempt at being sexy and just talked to him like he was a regular person.

We heard footsteps racing up the stairs and another crash from the hallway. The man's expression turned into panic and he reached for the doorknob. "I shouldn't be here," he said, like he just realized what he was doing was illegal.

He paused with his hand on the doorknob, ready to walk out. I was lying on the bed, pulling my nightgown back on, but as he turned to look at me, his eyes flashed to the belt mark on my stomach. It was red and raised, almost like a blister. He looked into my eyes, and I felt self-conscious about my dirty hair. "Fuck," he said, "You're just a kid, aren't you?"

I didn't say anything, because I couldn't. Because I didn't know who could hear.

The noise in the hallway escalated until we heard Candy scream, "NO! Please, God, no!"

The man glanced into the hallway and then back at me. "You aren't here because you want to be, are you?" he asked, like he was surprised I hadn't chosen this life.

I didn't say a word. I couldn't. I couldn't tell this man, who could possibly save my life, because I knew he wouldn't. If he saved my life, he would have to tell his wife why he saved a whore, and he wouldn't do that. If he saved my life, he would risk his own, and we both knew by looking at each other that the kind of man who rapes a young girl for pleasure isn't the kind of man who risks his life for anyone. Some people just aren't born good, I guess.

He glanced into the hallway again, mumbled *Fuck* under his breath, and ran out. With the door open, the screaming coming from Candy's room was louder.

"I can't go!" I heard her yell.

I heard skin hit skin, which I had come to recognize as the sound of someone being slapped in the face. I heard the stomp of boots and immediately thought of Angel's head against the ground. I heard another picture crash in the hall. *How many dumb flower pictures were there?*

"PLEASE!" Candy yelled again.

"Just pick her the fuck up!" It was Mike's voice. I thought he was gone today — I hadn't seen him, anyway — but, there he was.

I poked my head around the door to peek into the hallway. I didn't want anyone to catch me looking. I met Honey's eyes as she peeked around her door. The johns had bailed when they heard the noise. For men who think they can fuck someone without their consent, they get awfully scared when they think the police might be in the hallway.

She held her finger to her lips to tell me to be quiet. We watched as they dragged Candy out of her room, kicking, screaming, and turning every way she could. She grabbed onto the door frame and held on for dear life until one of Mike's men ripped her hands away and pinned them down by her sides. She twisted then and fell on her stomach. Her huge pregnant stomach hit the floor first and she cried out in pain.

"Get her the fuck up!" Mike shouted. He rarely looked panicked, but I saw a flash of *oh shit* move across his lips. He knew what he had just done. We all knew Candy's baby probably wouldn't survive whatever this was.

"PLEASE, Mike! PLEASE! I haven't done anything wrong!" Candy continued to scream.

"We gotta get her outta here, Mike," one of his men said.

"I know that, dipshit. Just pick her up."

All This Time in the Dark

When the man wrapped his arms around her chest and picked her up, I saw blood seeping into the back of her white nightgown. Part of me wanted to believe she was going to the hospital, that they had decided to give her and her baby the chance they deserved. A bigger part of me wondered if anyone would ever see her alive again.

"Careful!" Mike warned, as though Candy was precious cargo.

Candy kicked out, almost getting Mike in the legs. "I did everything you asked!" she screamed at him.

"We gotta get her downstairs. They have the car waiting."

"PLEASE! NO! Mike, they'll never find me. Nobody will ever find me."

Mike stopped and looked her dead in the eyes. We knew better than to look at Mike like that, but she stared right back at him as he whispered, "Nobody was ever going to find you, anyways, little girl. You were always my property. Don't you get that? You were always my fucking property."

Candy started sobbing and looked down at the ground. She didn't fight it when the men dragged her off downstairs. Mike trailed behind, talking on the phone as he went, "She's coming down. I can't guarantee the baby. Price is a thousand dollars, firm."

And that was all it took for me to realize that we could be measured in dollars. That our worth nothing more than a couple fucks and a thousand dollars. I went back and laid on my bed, hoping that, when it was my time to be sold, I would be worth more than a thousand dollars. I hoped that my life was worth more to someone than a small dollar sign and my ability to make some sick pervert happy in bed.

I rolled over and threw up in the trash can.

Kate

"Ian! Ian! Let me in!" I knew which bedroom was his. I hadn't knocked on the back door before, but the few times I had been to his house, he had always led me straight back to his room. I had never even more than the living room and Ian's room, like he was ashamed of the house or something.

His curtains pulled up and the light in his room clicked on.

"What the fuck?" he said, as he opened the window. "Kate? Is that you?"

"It's me!" I said. Haddie was standing a few feet behind me, hidden in the shadows. She refused to wait for me at the curb. We had walked here, just the two of us, alone in the dark. It had only taken twenty minutes, but walking uphill the whole way was awful.

"Kate, what are you doing?"

"I had to talk to you, Ian, and you weren't answering my phone calls."

"I didn't want to talk to you, Kate. I'm not good for you. You need to go be with someone who can give you what you want."

"Is this because I said I wanted sex?" I said.

All This Time in the Dark

"No, Kate, it's just —" he paused, sighed, and glanced over his shoulder, "— it's just that I can't be the guy you need. I can't. I care about you, Kate, and that's why I can't see you anymore."

"Ian, please! Please! I love you!"

"I have to go, Kate," he said, and he slammed the window shut.

I knocked again and, when he didn't answer, pounded on the window with my fist. "IAN!" I yelled.

He pulled open the window, "Kate! You're going to wake up my brother. You can't do this. Please, just go."

"But I love you. I miss you so much. I'm so sorry. Please, can't I just be your girlfriend again?"

"I don't know," he said, glancing behind him again.

"Kate, let's just go," Haddie whispered from the shadows.

"Who was that?" Ian said.

"It's just Haddie; she walked with me."

"You *walked* here?" Ian said.

"I can't drive, remember?" I hadn't gotten my license yet. It was embarrassing to be almost a senior without a license, but I also had waited too long to get my learners permit and was stuck driving with an adult for another two months.

"Kate, *please*," Haddie said.

I rolled my eyes. "Ian, please," I said through the window.

He hung his head down and looked at the floor. When he looked back up towards me, it looked like he was crying, "Okay. Alright, Kate. I'll call you tonight in, like, thirty minutes. Okay? My brother is getting ready to leave for work, and then I'll call you, I promise."

My heart fluttered and it felt like a weight had lifted from my chest. I felt relieved. "Okay! I'll wait by the phone. I love you, Ian." I blew him a kiss through the window and ran back to Haddie.

"Come on, Kate, I heard someone come out the front door," she said, yanking on my arm.

"It's probably just Ian's brother."

"We shouldn't be here," Haddie said. "This doesn't feel right."

I glanced back at the house and noticed a man leaning on the sill of a window in the upstairs portion of the house, where I had never been. He was staring right at us. As I turned to look at him, his face slowly spread into a smile. He lifted his hand and waved once.

"Okay, yeah, let's go," I said, and the whole way down the street, I could see the light on in the room upstairs. And, I swear, I could still see the man smiling at me.

Daisey

It has been a week since Candy has been gone. At least I think it has been a week. I haven't left my room except to go to the bathroom and, when I'm in there, I can't bring myself to look at the whiteboard on the wall.

Most of the time, I feel sick, like I need to puke, or I'm about to puke, and the rest of the time, I feel exhausted. I rarely have the energy or desire to make my clients happy, so Mike hasn't been very happy with me lately. It's a vicious cycle.

Another john comes in and sits on the edge of my bed. He starts to take off his tie. He smells like my father, and I wonder if they wear the same cologne. "Hey, baby," I say, without looking in his direction. I'm lying on my side, feeling like I want to throw up, barely moving. I know I've lost more weight the last few days, but I can't bring myself to eat anything other than one or two crackers at a time. If this is how I end, I don't really care. If this is all that's left for me, I don't really care.

I hear the man's wedding ring hit the table next to the door. They all always put their rings there. They can't forget them when they leave. "Roll over so I can see you," the man says. His voice sounds hoarse like he was yelling.

77

Maybe that's just how he sounds. *They sold Candy. They sold Candy. They sold Candy,* plays like a mantra in my mind. Maybe it's a warning, maybe it's just my mind in disbelief.

I roll over and wish I hadn't. The man is so huge, I wonder if he's going to break me. He easily weighs three hundred pounds, and he's a short little thing, squat and hairy like a Sasquatch. He's gross to look at, and yet he'll be inside me soon. I wonder if he's clean. It wouldn't be the first time someone like me has gotten AIDS or herpes. It's not like Mike is screening these men at the door. If they pay, they get in. I haven't heard what my rate is in a while, but I'm thinking that it has dropped pretty low. I'd be surprised if I was even worth $100 these days.

He climbs onto the bed, and I lie on my back and spread my legs. I am pale and lifeless. "Stand up," the man says. I do as I'm told. "Turn around," he says. I do. "Bend over," he orders. I do that, too. It's no use fighting anything. The Sasquatch can have me now.

He uses his mouth on me for a few minutes, and he makes noises like he likes it. I whimper in response. I don't have the energy to make the noises the men like. I don't have the energy to care if Mike kills me today or tomorrow or the next day. *He'll probably just sell you anyways,* I think. *You're too big of a liability if you're pregnant. Just like Candy was, remember? She was too big of a liability for them to keep anymore.* The man behind me stands up with his fat body and forces himself inside me from behind. I have a UTI, I'm sure of it and, when he pushes inside me, the burning is so bad, I cry out.

I got my first UTI back when I was in the room with Angel. She said I needed to pee right after sex, or it would burn like that. She also said having so many dicks in my body right in a row would do it, too. I can't remember a time when it hasn't burned lately.

"You like that, don't you?" The man says. He's a cliché. He bores me.

Candy is probably in Mexico by now, I think, while the man continues to thrust behind me. His dick is small, but it still burns.

All This Time in the Dark

You'll probably be in Mexico soon, too, I think. I feel a tear roll down my cheek. I don't bother to wipe it away. In the past four months, I have been doing the best that I can in the hopes that someday Mike will let me out. I've been keeping my head above water out of the fear that I don't want Mike to kill me. That if I can just do what these men say, I can make it out alive. But even if I make it out of this, if there is some chance of me surviving this, I know I won't be alive on the other side. I will be a half-empty, pregnant version of myself. No matter how many times I shower, or how many days go by, I will never be able to feel clean again. I will never be able to get this feeling off of me.

I lean onto the bed, my elbows feeling the combined weight of the fat man and myself. He's one of the ones who are too excited when they get here — he's already almost done. Tears roll down my cheeks and land on the bed in front of me. My dirty blanket, that has never been washed the whole time I have been here, has small wet dots on it. I don't care if the man behind me sees.

He screams when he cums. It's annoying. He sounds stupid. He finished inside me, which is not new to me. I guess it's how I got in this situation in the first place. The men downstairs hand every guy a condom when they come in. Some of them use them, some of them don't. We aren't supposed to ask. That's not our job. The roll of paper towels that sits on the table by the door is a gift from Mike. Every room has a roll of paper towels. Sometime in the night, when we're asleep, a new roll is placed on the table. Every night. Like a gift from Santa. The man grabs a handful and uses it to clean himself.

"You were great, baby," he says like I even did anything. I was just a doll in his charade.

I climb back up on the bed and roll over onto my side again. I face away from him. He slides his ring back on, buttons his pants, and leaves, closing the door behind him. When he's gone, I grab some of the paper towels and shove them into my crotch. I don't want to go to the bathroom, but I also don't want him leaking out of me onto my bed. So, I just lay there, tears rolling down my face, with paper towels shoved between my legs.

The bed is itchy, the covers scratchy. My nightgown is dirty and it stinks. A few nights ago, after Candy left, someone left a new, clean white nightgown on the floor inside my room. I don't know who it was from, but it looks like the one Candy wore, and I can't bear to wear it. I can't bear to do anything. I'm tired, and every piece of me hurts.

Kate

I think Ian and I are back together, but it's not the same as it was before. He is distant and moody, and he never calls when he says he will, which is the worst feeling in the world. I finally realize what Jovie is always talking about when she says men are assholes. I never believed her until Ian kept saying he would call, and then he didn't.

But the problem is I love him, and it's true love. I fully believe Ian and I will end up married one day because *how could we not?* It's just a rough patch, honestly. It's not like the true Ian is an asshole. It's like the true Ian is somewhere hiding, and I'm just trying to find him. *I can help make him better,* I keep thinking. But for some strange reason, that never seems to work out.

I miss the old Ian. I miss holding his hand as we walked down the hallway at school. He won't kiss me, either. Not since we've been back together. He just chooses not to. I asked him if I smelled bad once. He said no, but he also laughed when he said it, so I don't know if I believe him. I asked Haddie if she thought there was something wrong with me, but she always says no, that it must be Ian. I guess I have to agree with her, but I can't when I love him so much.

After the first time we snuck out of the house to go to Ian's house, we found it was easier than we always thought it would be. My parents didn't notice our empty bedrooms or our footsteps on the stairs. When they were asleep in their room, with the door shut, they were deaf to the rest of the house. The problem was they trusted us when maybe they shouldn't have. Or, rather, maybe they should have just kept a better eye on us. Or slept with their door open.

Either way, Haddie and I simply did whatever it was we wanted to do that summer. Because we could. Because our parents trusted us and didn't ask a lot of questions. And, when they did ask questions, we were smart enough to give them the answers they wanted.

We started sneaking out at night a few times a week. At first, it was just to go to a few parties. Our curfew was eleven o'clock on weeknights, even in the summer, but the senior cheerleaders threw parties at two a.m. Haddie and I found that life after eleven o'clock was infinitely better than life before eleven, and we decided we had missed out on too much by sticking to that stupid curfew. Once we started getting away from the house, there was no stopping us.

We spent the nights laughing and playing, sometimes drinking. Those nights were the nights Haddie and I had gotten so close, it felt like our bond would be unbreakable forever.

"You and Haddie have gotten so close. I love to see it," my mom said one morning. We had fallen asleep together in Haddie's room after spending the entire night at Jovie's house. Her parents had been out of town and we had the place to ourselves. We didn't do anything except play Truth or Dare and skinny dip in her parent's pool. Jovie dared us to go streaking down her street, but it was so cold the three of us only made it a few houses before we ran back inside laughing until we couldn't breathe.

"Yeah, Mom," I had said, slightly annoyed. She always had to get in our business, and she ruined the fun if she did.

All This Time in the Dark

"I just think it's nice that you two can be so close."

I had rolled my eyes because she sounded ridiculous and I didn't have time for it. Those few weeks of summer with Haddie, we had never felt freer or more alive. It was like the entire world was our own, and we could explore it and arrange it however we wanted to. The best part was, even though Ian left me alone more often than not, I found that Haddie never did. Haddie, even with her midriff tops and glitter-painted fingernails, was more loyal than most. She was funny and engaging, and I genuinely liked her as a person. Which surprised me because I hadn't really ever noticed her before.

"Ian's calling," I said one night as we laid together in my bed. On the nights we stayed home and didn't sneak out, we would often watch movies together or spend time on Facebook together laughing and talking. We could spend hours just talking about nothing.

Haddie paused, "What? Didn't he say he would call at seven?"

"Yeah, I guess he thought that meant ten-thirty."

"Are you going to answer?"

"I guess. He's my boyfriend, isn't he?"

She shrugged, looking irritated. She sat up and crossed her arms.

"Hey," I said to Ian.

"Hey, Kate. Sorry I didn't call earlier. I was working for my brother."

"Yeah, you've been saying that a lot," I answered back, and then hit the speaker button so Haddie could hear him, too. She relaxed and uncrossed her arms, certain that, for the time being, I was safe.

"Sorry," Ian said, annoyed.

"Well, what are you up to?"

"Just thinking about you," he said. I blushed.

"I'm thinking about you, too," I said. Haddie rolled her eyes.

"It was fun the other night."

"At the party?"

"Yeah."

"I don't remember too much," I admitted, almost embarrassed that I'd had so much to drink. Haddie hadn't had anything to drink that night. As we'd walked home in the warm summer night, her arm linked through mine, I had rested my head on her shoulder. Her deep black curls kept getting in my mouth and I thought it was hilarious that I had to keep spitting them out. It never occurred to me until that night that I had missed having a relationship with my sister.

"You seemed pretty excited in Cam's room."

Haddie looked at me and raised her eyebrows. Cam. Cameron Stone. The guy whose house we had been at. He was about to be a senior in the fall. He was somewhat popular, but only because his parents had money and left him alone a lot. He wasn't popular because he was likeable. But, then again, most people who are popular aren't that likable. They're just good at getting people to follow them.

"I guess I was," I said back.

"Maybe we can repeat that sometime," Ian said.

My heart started racing. Even though he was being a jerk these past few weeks, I still wanted to have sex with him. I basically wanted to have sex with anybody because I was almost seventeen, and I didn't want to start my senior year as a virgin.

"Yeah, I'd like that."

"Tomorrow night?" He whispered.

"Yes. Pick me up at midnight."

"Got it," he said.

"Hey, Ian?"

"What?"

"I love you."

"You, too, Kate."

All This Time in the Dark

My hands were sweating as I hung up the phone. Haddie looked concerned. Her eyebrows were furrowed together, and her head was down. Her curls fell over her face. She crossed her arms again.

"Kate, I don't think you're making a smart move here."

"Nobody asked you, Had. My body, my choice."

"I don't think that means what you think it means."

"I think it means I can sleep with whoever I want to."

"I'm not saying you can't, I'm just saying be careful."

"Haddie, you turn sixteen next week, this is adult stuff. I don't expect you to know anything about falling in love and wanting to share that love with your boyfriend. Do you even know anything about sex?" I knew she knew a little bit, after eavesdropping on her phone calls, but I didn't expect her head to snap up like she was angry when I said it.

When her eyes met mine, her cheeks were red and her eyes brimmed with tears. "I know more than you think."

"Haddie," I said, stunned. I lowered my voice, "Haddie, are you a virgin?"

"I don't know, Kate. I don't know what I would call myself."

"What's that mean? Either you've had sex, or you haven't."

"It's not that simple," she said. I saw one tear slide quietly down her face. It settled on the neckline of her baby blue tank top.

"Haddie?"

"I didn't have sex because I wanted too, Kate. I didn't have a choice."

"What does that mean?" I realized I was suddenly scared. I was scared for my sister and what she was about to say. I was scared for myself. I was scared that the summer we had enjoyed so much was about to be ruined by one single revelation.

"I had sex with Joe a few months ago. But, Kate, I told him I didn't want to have sex with him. I swear I told him no. But he drove me home one night after I stayed out too late and drank a little too much, and I felt like I had to do it. I felt like I didn't have a choice because he ran his hand up my leg and said I shouldn't be wearing such a short skirt if I didn't want to. I kind of wanted to, I guess, but I wasn't even dating him, and I always thought my first time would be with someone I really liked. And when he started, you know, I just didn't know how to stop him. So, I just laid there."

"Haddie, that's… that's rape."

"No, I don't think so, Kate. Joe said it wasn't, and when I told some of the girls, they were excited for me because I wasn't a virgin anymore. So, I think it's okay, Kate, I think it is. I don't know if I even count it as sex because it only lasted, like, five minutes and I didn't really want to do it."

"Haddie, you should tell Mom. Joe should be in trouble for this."

"No! Kate! You can't tell anyone. Joe told me not to. He said he would be in trouble with his parents if they found out. I promised him I wouldn't say anything to anyone or that anyone would find out, and he believed me. He felt so bad when it was over, Kate. He felt horrible. He knew we shouldn't have done it."

"Haddie! You had been drinking and he took advantage of you! You're only fifteen years old! Joe is seventeen! He knows better!" I was panicked, and the fear in my voice couldn't be masked. I hated that this had happened to Haddie. I hated that I couldn't stop it. I hated that there was nothing either of us could do.

"Kate, please. I can't have the school find out about this. If the guys find out, they'll just call me a slut. You know how they are. As soon as the girls at school start having sex, they're labeled as 'easy' and all the men think they're ready for a good time. I can't be one of those girls. I just want to get through high school."

"But Haddie!" I yelled.

"Shhhhh, Kate, please! Please don't say anything. I'm okay now, I promise. After it happened, I was a mess for a few days, but I'm better now. I promise. It was just a stupid incident. Nothing like that will ever happen again.

All This Time in the Dark

Joe was probably right, I mean, I did wear a pretty short skirt. And it's not like I tried to push him off of me. I said no a couple of times and then finally just laid there. So, he was probably right, I guess."

I started crying — more out of fear for my sister than anything else. I was afraid that her sweet voice could be silenced so easily. I was afraid that one day she would look back and realize that what she had gone through wasn't a normal experience. That her saying "no" to a boy in a car should have been enough. I was afraid that she would grow up thinking she owed men things because they had gotten in a car and driven her somewhere. I was afraid she would grow up thinking sex was something to be owed, instead of something to be enjoyed. In that moment, she looked so small, like I could carry her around in my arms. I didn't know how to help her. She seemed embarrassed, like what happened had been her fault. It broke my heart into five thousand pieces.

I remembered one Easter when she had gotten a stuffed bunny in her basket. It was brown, and she named it Bunny. It was soft and sweet with blue bows tied around its ears. I had asked her why she needed to carry a stuffed bunny when she was seven years old.

"You're too old for that," I had teased her.

"It just makes me feel safe, Kate," she had said. But I'd teased her enough that she finally put the bunny on a shelf in her room and never picked it up again. I felt terrible when she set it down; I had never meant for her not to have it. I was just being a mean big sister.

But, sitting on my bed that night, listening to Haddie describe what was definitely rape to me, made me realize that, just like she had set her bunny down without a fight, she had laid her own body on the line to avoid any conflict. She wanted to put her rape on a shelf and never pick it up again, and she was asking me to let her.

Daisey

I stopped eating a few days back and never found the interest in starting again. Food didn't taste good and I stopped caring if I was dead or not. It just didn't matter. I could tell I had lost even more weight. I figured if I ever made it home, nobody would recognize me anyways, so what was the point in even trying to get there.

      Since I had stopped eating, I had also stopped trying to decide if I was pregnant. I figured I still was. I had yet to write my name on the whiteboard, but a part of me hoped I could starve the thing right out of me. Even if I did have a baby, I didn't know what I would tell it when it got older. *You'll never know your father because he paid to rape me.* I couldn't even guess who the father might have been. My parents wouldn't want a whore's baby living in their house. I wouldn't know how to take care of it.

      Sometimes, when I was lying in bed just staring at the ceiling, I reminded myself that I was only eighteen years old. I guessed I was closer to eighteen now. Now that I had been here for so long. But I couldn't be so sure. I missed days. I didn't have a calendar and didn't have a pen, so I had no way to keep track of time. The worst part was that I couldn't see anything outside,

All This Time in the Dark

beyond the bars and the tops of the trees I could barely make out. I could see the light shine in during the day and sometimes the moonlight at night, and that was all. It could be Christmas, and I would have no idea.

The rape never stopped. We never got days off.

The johns I entertained stopped being as interested in me when I stopped caring whether I lived. A sick part of me hoped Mike would kill me because then I could die quickly rather than live the long, hard life of a whore. Some of the girls whispered that Candy was taken to Mexico. I didn't doubt it. The men who took her were speaking a different language and Mexico was closest. Maybe she crossed the border up to Canada. Maybe she got free in an airport somewhere.

When I was six years old, my parents had taken me to Las Vegas for the weekend. I don't remember much of the trip, but I had just started reading, and I remember sitting down to pee in the bathroom, and there was a sign that said the airport was a Safe Place and to report sex trafficking. I don't remember anything about the airplane ride, but I remember asking my mother what that sign meant. She was as honest with me as she could be: "Some women and children are taken and sold and forced to do things they don't want to do," she had said. It sounded horrible to me back then.

I was one of them now.

Mike could tell I wasn't his best girl anymore. I don't know if I really ever had been, but there was a time when he complimented me a lot, and the food he gave me was actually kind of good. He used to send in the better guys; most of them smelled good and were married. The married ones were always ones I trusted more because it meant they at least had someone — maybe even kids — back at home. I don't know if everyone is bad. Maybe some people were just so desperate for love that they came to me. That's the way I used to justify it when the men were married. The johns I got now were getting scarier by the day, and I figured it was because they were the ones who couldn't pay as much. Mike was getting bored with me.

"Daisey," Mike said one night when he came to sit on the edge of my bed. Some of the girls said he had sex with them regularly, but he had never had sex with me. Not yet anyways.

I didn't answer him. Daisey wasn't my name. I was sick of hearing it.

"Daisey girl, you're not making me any money."

I glanced in his direction but didn't say anything. If I wasn't throwing up, I was feeling dizzy. I didn't have the energy to do anything anymore.

"You need to snap out of this. You're stuck here. Might as well make the most of it."

I shrugged and stared at the floor.

Mike grabbed my arm and pushed his fingers around on the inside of my elbow. When I looked at what he was doing, he looked like the lady at my doctor's office when she was looking for a vein to take my blood. I had only had my blood taken once, but it looked the same. He tied something around my arm, bounced his fingers on the vein he found a few times, and slowly and confidently slipped a needle under my skin.

"This will give you some energy," he said.

"What is it?" I mumbled.

"Don't worry about it."

I felt a rush to my head and the room started to spin. I don't remember what happened next.

Daisey

A full day went by, and I couldn't remember anything. One of the other girls said they saw me running up and down the hall screaming like a crazy person. Another girl said I came into her room and wouldn't stop scratching at my face. She said I told her there were bugs crawling on me. I don't remember that. I don't remember anything.

I know Mike gives some of the girls heroin or cocaine on a regular basis. That's why girls like Angel came here in the first place. Mike is a criminal, but he isn't a liar. I guess those two don't have to go hand in hand, even though maybe they should. Maybe it would be easier to condemn criminals if they were always lying when they did it. If Mike says he'll give you coke or speed in exchange for fucking, then we all know he will. I don't know what drug Mike gave me. One of the girls said she was sure it was cocaine because the first few times she did it herself, it gave her the feeling of being crawled all over. Another girl just came up behind me and whispered *meth* into my ear super creepy-like, and that scared me.

When I was in middle school, we had a special assembly where all four hundred of us eighth graders piled into the gymnasium to listen to a police officer talk about how bad drugs were. He called himself the DARE officer and said he was "daring" us to stay away from drugs. He acted like when we got into high school, people would be just standing outside the school, handing us bags of cocaine. I don't remember everything he said, because we were all bored and passing notes, but he did say meth was bad and doing meth once would be like running headfirst into the brick wall of the gym over and over again. It scared me at the time, and I didn't know why.

That same police officer had asked anybody who was willing to never do drugs, even in high school, to stand up and take an oath. Then he gave us dog tags that said *DARE* on them. I remember a kid named Jeremy refused to stand up and take the oath, and the entire class talked about it the next day. As far as I know, Jeremy is still in school, but he regularly smokes behind the gas station across the street at lunch every day. None of us were surprised, given that he was probably already doing drugs. Otherwise, he would have stood up and lied like the rest of us. Of course, none of us really wanted to do drugs back then, but we also couldn't guarantee that we would never try them. But our teachers were watching, and if we didn't stand up, they would look at us funny like they looked at Jeremy.

In seventh grade, I took my oath seriously, and I wore my dog tags every day. Once everyone in high school started experimenting with weed and alcohol every weekend, I silently slipped my dog tags into the garbage. I was embarrassed to wear something so childish when everyone around me wasn't scared of a little pot. I guess it was a good thing I threw them away now, anyways, since I had fucked over a hundred random men and been shot up with either meth, cocaine, or heroin. Probably all three. And whatever else they gave me when they thought I was Angel and almost died. Those dog tags meant jack shit now. I wonder if the DARE officer would count what I had done as "doing drugs" when I never did them willingly or even knew what I was taking.

When I finally came to my senses after a day of not remembering running down the hall stark naked, Mike was sitting on the edge of my bed,

All This Time in the Dark

rubbing my leg. Maybe we'd had sex when I was out of it and just didn't know it. I had stopped looking at Mike like the bad guy a long time ago, and simply thought he was another person just trying to make it in this world. Maybe it was like that one Lifetime movie I watched a while ago where the main girl fell in love with her captor, and everyone said it was Stockholm Syndrome, but we all knew it was probably just true love. Maybe Mike and I were in love forever. Or maybe he just needed someone to fuck. Either way, I couldn't fight it.

"You're awake," he said, staring into my eyes. I wondered if this would be the day he sent me to Mexico.

"I guess," I croaked out, my voice sounding raspy.

"Daisey girl, are you pregnant?" Mike asked me.

I didn't know what to say, because I didn't know if it was true. I didn't know how to answer a question I didn't have the answer to. So, I just shrugged.

"I think you might be pregnant," Mike said.

"Why?"

He sighed and ran a hand through his hair. If he lost twenty pounds and stopped capturing young girls, he might even be attractive, "One of the girls told me."

My face flushed red and my hands started to shake. I couldn't believe one of the girls who had said they were a friend to me would rat me out like that. I thought we were all in this together. I guess I was fucking wrong. "I don't really know," I finally answered, still without looking him in the eye. Always without looking him in the eye.

"I can't say it's a good thing if you are."

I shrugged. I looked down at my stomach. It looked so hollow, so empty. My hip bones poked out from the front of my nightgown. My knees were knobby. My skin was so pale I could see all the veins running through my body. I didn't look like anything other than sick.

Mike tossed two boxes onto the bed next to me. "Use these. If you are, I can use it for a few months and get some extra money. Pregnant girls sell."

Tessa M. Osborne

I blushed. I didn't know why I blushed, but I did. I didn't want Mike to know anything personal about me. I was embarrassed in front of the man who literally sold my virginity for seven hundred dollars.

He walked out of the room and I sat on the bed with the boxes in my hand. I stared at them for a long time. I wasn't sure what they were at first — I had never needed to buy anything like that before. But then it slowly dawned on me that Mike had handed me two boxes with pregnancy tests inside, and he expected me to take them and then report back. They didn't look like the kind I had seen at Target. They were a generic brand, not First Response or the fancy digital ones I had held with Jovie. She needed one once. I was the person she called to go with her to buy them. She said the digital ones were expensive, so they were probably the best. I remember standing in the aisle at Target next to her, giggling at the different boxes, wondering which one would be good for her to try. She cried when it was negative.

I didn't know how to take them. I didn't know what I was supposed to do. I thought about myself ten years older, married, happy. I would come home from work one day, from a job that I loved, with a grocery bag swinging on my arm. I would run upstairs and excitedly take the pregnancy test. While I waited for the results, I would see the diamond ring on my finger glisten in the light. I would smile and maybe cry. I would be so excited about that positive result. My husband would get home, and I would hand him the test, and we would cry together, and pick out colors for our nursery, and think of names while we laid in bed together. We would be in love and I would be safe.

But right now, I didn't know who to turn to. I didn't know if anyone around me was safe. I missed my mother. I wished she were here so I could ask her how to do this. Like when I got my first period and we sat over the toilet together while I tried to figure out how to stick a pad to my underwear. She would help me now like she helped me then. She would help me turn the test the right way and tell me how long to wait. She would tell me what the results meant. She would cry with me and hug me and I would feel safe.

All This Time in the Dark

Instead, I lifted my tired, emaciated eighteen-year-old body up off the bed I had fucked in over and over again and dragged myself down the hall toward the bathroom I shared with six other sex slaves. I carried the boxes — that I didn't buy — by the corners. I didn't want to touch them. I stared at the ground and, when Honey said my name, I kept walking and didn't turn to her. I didn't know if she was the one who had told Mike. Angel wouldn't have done that to me.

I trudged into the bathroom and locked the door. I always doubted if the lock even worked. It shouldn't. How would Mike know we were okay in there. How would he know if we were ever going to come out? I sat down on the toilet and rubbed my hands over the small injection marks on my arms — the one from yesterday was sore, while the ones from when Angel was alive had faded to scars.

Using all my strength, I ripped open the first box. It was bright pink and just said the words PREGNANCY TEST in big, bold letters on the front. I thought about all the women who bought pregnancy tests and hoped for a positive. I wondered if any of them had been raped like I had been. *I mean it's not really rape*, I always told myself, *Mike always reminds you that it isn't rape. You didn't actually say no, remember?*

I threw the box into the trash can. I read the instructions three different times to make sure I took the test right. I didn't care about getting an accurate result for Mike; I wanted to get an accurate result for me, so I would know if I wanted to die. The directions said to wait for three minutes before reading the result, but I didn't have a clock. So, I counted to sixty three different times. I cried the entire time I was counting. By the time I was done, my nose was running, and I had to dry my eyes to see the test right.

I glanced down at the test, afraid to look at it all the way. Two small pink lines show up, and they just sat there looking at me, like two pink snake eyes. I took the second test because I had to be sure I knew the answer. I didn't know if false positives were a thing, but if they were, I just needed to know for sure. I counted to sixty again, three times, and peeked at the test with one eye, thinking maybe I could trick my brain into just seeing one line instead of two, but there they were: two tiny pink lines. The directions said that meant I was pregnant. I dropped the test to the ground, and it broke into two pieces. The piece I had peed on slid behind the toilet somewhere. I didn't bother picking it up.

    Before I left the bathroom, I walked over to the whiteboard on the wall. I wrote my name and added a line for the next five days. It didn't matter if it was true. I refused to give Mike any more control over my body. I would hide this pregnancy, even if it killed me.

Kate

I hadn't seen Ian since the night I snuck off to his house. We made plans to meet each other again, and I spent the entire week waiting and waiting for that night to come. It couldn't come fast enough. Haddie had said she wanted to come with me again; she didn't like Ian and didn't feel safe with me going to meet him alone.

I wanted to have sex with Ian. I felt like we were both ready. And even if we didn't have a relationship afterwards, I just wanted to be in the same club as Haddie and Jovie. I wanted to be like the other cheerleaders at the school. I wanted to be confident and happy and know that no matter what boy looked my way, I could meet him evenly on the playing field. I wanted the experience.

The night I was going to meet Ian again, Haddie and I had the whole thing planned. I was going to go to bed early and she would wait thirty minutes before joining me. We said we would wait in my room until our parents clicked the living room TV off and finally went up to their room. It was foolproof; we had done it enough that summer to know what we were doing. The difference was, this night, Haddie had promised to give Ian and me time alone. We were going to meet Ian at a party down the road and she promised she would wait outside wherever we went in and keep an eye out for anything that looked weird. I was sure the only place we would end up going would be the back seat of his car. I didn't want to tell Haddie that she was too young and small to stop anything bad from happening to me, but I liked that she was concerned.

Ian had made it clear in our text messages that he was going to have sex with me. Or at least get close. *I can't wait to finally have you naked*, he had written. *I can't believe we waited so long.*

I don't know what it was, but something had changed in who he was and what he wanted from me. It was a relief. I was relieved that he wanted me back. I was relieved to be wanted. I finally felt like I belonged with the other cheerleaders, like someone other than the smart girl who was good at school and student council. I didn't feel like I knew anything about boys yet, I hadn't even seen a penis in real life, but I was sure I could handle whatever situation Ian and I found ourselves in.

But the night Haddie and I were going to meet Ian, Haddie got sick. I thought it was probably just the Mexican food she had eaten earlier, but she thought she had a stomach virus. Haddie couldn't stop throwing up, and she looked all pale and sweaty. She told me she could still try and come with me, but I figured it would be better if she stayed home. Nobody wanted anybody throwing up at a party. Besides, I knew I wouldn't need her help; nothing would happen to me as long as Ian was there.

"I still want to go, Kate. I don't think this is a good idea."

"We'll be at a party, Had, nothing is going to happen to me."

"I don't trust him."

"We'll be with hundreds of other people, I'm sure."

"Don't leave the party with him," Haddie begged, "Please, Kate, please don't leave the party with him."

"I won't," I promised Haddie. I kissed the top of her head and turned off her bedroom light. The glow from the TV lit up her bed. She looked so small and young lying there, so tired like life had already been hard on her. I knew she would be okay — she was a fighter — but I hoped that one-day justice would be served for what had happened to her. I just didn't know if the world worked that way or not.

I'm on my way, Ian finally texted an hour later. My stomach was anxious, my heart about to beat out of my chest.

I will leave now and walk down to the party, I answered.

Just meet me down the street. I don't want to go to a party.

Where are we going to go?

Let's go somewhere, just the two of us.

I remembered Haddie's warning and the promise I had made to her. If I left with Ian, Haddie would kill me. But the next day, when I came back into Haddie's room with my grand adventure under my belt, she would understand. She would know that I wasn't her, and that Ian and I had made love — because we *both* wanted to — and we were madly in love with each other. She would know that we *both* wanted to be together

Somewhere alone sounds perfect, I wrote back.

Ian sent back the smiley face emoji with a thumbs up and a heart. Since we weren't going to the party, I didn't bother putting my cute clothes on. Instead, I slipped on a nice pair of underwear — ones that were young, cute, and girlish with *Hello Kitty* on the front. I put on clean shorts and the first t-shirt I pulled out of my drawer. I figured he would want to just take it off of me anyways.

I waved goodbye to Haddie before I snuck out. She was still awake but looked like she would drift away at any second.

"Nice shirt," she said as I turned around to leave.

I glanced down at my blue shirt with the cats on it, "Thanks," I said, "Gramma gave it to me."

Part Three

Part Three

Haddie

The first week after Kate went missing everybody cried. Anybody who had even met her once would stop me and tell me how much they missed her. They would say she had a good heart and then add some bullshit about her being funny or something. I never know how to respond to that because Kate wasn't really that funny.

The second week, the school held a memorial for her, like she had died, even though nobody knew if that was true. The girls who had known her or had taken a class with her, had maybe brushed her shoulder in the hallway, all posted about her on their Facebook pages. Some of them had the balls to post her picture on their Instagram pages and say how they had known her and were so sad she was gone. I thought that was bullshit.

By the fourth week, school had gone back to normal and no one said her name anymore, although someone had started a Blue Ribbon campaign in her honor, hanging bright blue string up all over town to remind everyone that Kate was gone and needed to be found. By the time she had been gone a month, the ribbons started to flutter to the ground in the wind. My English teacher complained one day about how nobody was ever going to pick all those ribbons up. I guess that is all Kate was anymore — someone who had fluttered away. Someone nobody wanted to take credit for anymore.

My parents told me I didn't have to go to school, but my mom cried all day long, and my dad was going to work like nothing was wrong, so going to school seemed better than that. At least at school I could see my friends and Kate's friends, and we could talk about her together. Or, even better, not talk about her at all. Besides, at school, the teachers didn't expect much from me. I was the girl whose sister had gone missing. They thought all I should do is show up and sit there, so I got all As just by walking in the door.

Since no one knew what had happened to her, I spent my junior year of high school trying to figure it out. It felt better to wondering than to feel nothing at all. Originally, I wondered if Ian would know what had happened. He was supposed to have met her that night, and we all counted on his story. At first, Ian would show up at the house every day. Some people said they saw him out with the search parties they set up around town. Some people said they saw him swimming in the river, calling out her name. Some even said they saw him crying. I never saw any of that, though. He showed up at the house for a few weeks, and then he drifted away, just like the ribbons around town. When the news ran stories on Kate, they usually showed pictures of her with Ian. A news station even interviewed him asking whoever had her to just bring her home. It didn't feel right to me; it seemed staged.

The police questioned him after Kate went missing. He told me once that they kept coming to his house and even talked to his brother and uncle to confirm where he had been that night. He still said he had been at the party looking for Kate, but never found her so, eventually, just went home. They seemed curious at first since Ian was the guy who had maybe raped Taylor O'Donnell, but they eventually got bored and left it alone. I always wished they would have dug deeper. Maybe they were missing something. Maybe we all were.

All This Time in the Dark

I hated myself every day for not going with Kate the night she left. If I had gone with her, this might never have happened. I knew something was wrong the night she left. I wished I would have stopped her from leaving. I wished so much that everything had been different. A part of me had felt she wouldn't come home if she left. I even texted her as she was leaving the house, but she never answered me. The police found her phone in front of the neighbor's house in the gutter. The detectives on Kate's case think she dropped it, but sometimes I think maybe someone left it there so she wouldn't be found.

Missing Kate comes in waves. Big ones, usually, that crash against my chest at night when I'm trying to sleep and make it hard to breathe. There's always a few moments, when I've just woken up from a dream and I'm lying in bed between sleep and wakefulness, when I feel so normal, like my brain hasn't caught up with anything that's wrong, and it still thinks that everything is right. And then I remember that Kate is gone, and my brain must relive her disappearance all over again. Those are the moments that it hurts to breathe. When I remember what it was like to wake up and realize that her room was empty.

"KATE!" That's how I woke up the morning after Kate went missing, to my mother shouting her name and frantically running from room to room.

"KATE!" my father shouted outside. He checked to see if the cars were gone. It wasn't like Kate to take a car since she didn't have a driver's license, but my parents also didn't think it was like Kate to sneak out at night, and I guess that happened. Both cars were parked at home.

I felt like I was going to shit myself as I heard them yelling Kate's name. A part of me simply thought Kate had spent the night at Ian's and lost track of time. I hoped that she would come into the house, guilty and worried at eight in the morning. Maybe she actually *had* had sex with him and had fallen asleep.

When my parents had realized she wasn't anywhere in the house, they tore into my room, not caring that I was still sick with food poisoning and had spent the better part of the day before throwing up.

"Haddie! Haddie! Wake up! Where is she? Where's your sister?"

It sounded like they were accusing me of hiding her, like I would lift up my covers, and there she would be, under my comforter. "I don't know," I had said, pulling the covers over my head.

"She's not here, Haddie! She's gone!" My mother answered, pulling the covers down from my face.

"I don't know where she is!" I said, smacking my mom's hand away and sitting up.

"Where could she have gone, Haddie?"

I swung my legs over the edge of the bed and sat up higher to face my parents head-on. "The last time I saw her, she was sneaking out to go meet Ian."

My mother burst into tears, "What do you mean she was sneaking out to meet Ian?"

"I'm so sorry, Mom. We've been sneaking out all summer." I don't know why I found it necessary to tell my mother I had also been breaking her rules, but I still hoped Kate was coming home, and I thought maybe we could be in this together.

"Where is she?! Tell me right now, Haddie!"

"I don't know. She was meeting Ian at Tyler's party down the street. That's all I know."

"Tyler Martin?" my father asked from behind my mother. "You mean the Martin family down the road?"

"Yeah, I guess."

He left the room. I heard him on the phone a few minutes later, talking to someone. It sounded like a lot of questioning about a party, and then he finally said, "Are your parents' home?" Everyone at school knew Tyler's parents were out of town. I figured his parents would probably find out about the party now. I felt bad for Tyler.

"Where would she go, Haddie?" my mother asked. She still had tears in her eyes. I felt bad for letting her down. I felt like it was my fault.

"I don't know. All she told me was she was leaving to go meet Ian at Tyler's party. She told me she was going to walk down to Tyler's house, and Ian would meet her there. She promised me she wouldn't leave the party."

"Where else have you two been going this summer?"

"Usually just to friends' houses. Honest. We haven't gone anywhere else. Sometimes there's just a party that lasts later than our curfew, and we know you wouldn't let us go."

"I don't let you do those kinds of things because it isn't safe. Because I was afraid that one day you wouldn't come home. You aren't invincible, Haddie."

"Mom, we just go to our friends' houses. I wouldn't be stupid enough to go anywhere else."

"Tyler said he never saw Kate last night. You've never gone anywhere else?" my dad asked, appearing behind my mom. He must have been done on the phone. He looked pissed.

"Well, I mean, one time we did."

"Where did you go, Haddie?" My dad was yelling at this point and my mother was crying again.

"I went with Kate to Ian's house."

"Call Ian's house *now*," Mom whispered to Dad. I figured that was coming. I had hoped it would be safe to assume that Kate had accidentally spent the night over there. I had hoped that when they picked up the phone to call Ian's house, Kate would wake up and realize what she had done.

I heard my dad on the phone again, talking to someone else. He sounded the way he did when he spoke to other adult men. His voice always got deeper, and he called them "bro" a lot, like they had some brotherhood that the rest of us didn't understand because we weren't men.

He came back into the room. "Ian's brother, Mike, said Kate isn't there. I talked to Ian, also, and he said he never saw Kate last night."

"That's impossible," I said. "She told me she was leaving to meet him. She wanted to… well, just, I don't know." I regretted the words as they came out of my mouth. I had been about to speak without thinking. Kate said I did that a lot.

"To what, Haddie?"

"I don't know."

"You're lying."

"Kate's the one missing, but I'm the one on trial?"

"Tell the truth."

"This isn't fair!"

"Haddie, tell us now!"

"Fine! She wanted to lose her virginity last night. Are you happy now?"

My father's cheeks turned red, like he had never heard of sex before, and my mother gasped. "Kate wouldn't do that," my mom said.

I shrugged.

We all sat there staring at each other for a few minutes, not sure what to say. Kate had told me she was going to go meet Ian; Ian said he never saw her. Tyler said he never saw her. I heard her footsteps in the driveway last night. *So where did she go?*

"Did you call her cell phone?" I finally said, breaking the silence.

"Of course, we called her cell phone, Haddie," my mom said. I could tell she thought I was stupid.

"Did you call Jovie?" I asked.

"I'll call her family now," my dad said and left again.

All This Time in the Dark

"I don't believe Kate would want to do that," my mom said. I guess she'd never thought that her daughters would one day have sex. She was always open and honest with us about sex, but she also made it clear that we should only do it if we were in love.

"Kate is in love with him, Mom."

She glared at me. I laid back on my bed and looked up at my ceiling. My stomach rolled, and I realized I had forgotten that I wasn't feeling well. "And what about you, Haddie?" she said, "Have you been having sex?"

My entire body turned red and my head felt like it was on fire. Even if I tried to lie, my Mom would be able to tell I was lying because I was red everywhere. "I mean... I have had sex before," I finally mumbled, refusing to meet her gaze.

"Oh, Haddie," my mom sat back.

"I'm sorry, Mom, it was a stupid mistake."

"You're only fifteen!"

"I'll be sixteen next week."

"You're too young to be doing this."

"I'm not as young as you think I am anymore, Mom."

"How many boys, Haddie?"

"Just one."

"Were you safe?"

"Like, you mean, did we use a condom?"

"Yes, that's exactly what I mean." She sounded so disgusted with me, it made my stomach hurt more. I could tell she thought I was damaged now, that I had done something wrong.

My father came around the corner then, "What? You mean what, Jess?" he asked.

"It seems as if our daughter is having sex, Robert, that's what I mean."

"She what? Which daughter?"

"Haddie."

"What the hell, Jessica? I don't want to know that!"

I looked at both of my parents. They were still young — my Mom was only thirty-eight. She dressed young, looked young, acted young. At school, people knew her as the cool mom. Cool, but strict. She was beautiful and funny. She liked bright colors and, at my eighth-grade graduation, three different thirteen-year-old boys had asked me if she was my older sister. Her bright pink dress that night had gotten their attention in the way most middle school boys notice hot women. But she was acting differently now. Older.

"Mom, how old were you when you first had sex?"

I saw my father glance at her, and she looked down at the ground. I wondered if they'd ever had that conversation. I was sure they did. Didn't all married people have conversations like that?

"I was fifteen," she finally whispered.

"Don't tell her that!" my Dad said. He still looked mad.

"I can't lie to her," Mom answered.

"I don't think any of this is important right now. Where is Kate?"

They turned and left my bedroom. They didn't talk to me for the rest of the day, not when a police officer knocked on the door, not when the detective showed up and questioned us in separate bedrooms for hours, not when the cadaver dogs came and combed the house. Not when Kate's cell phone was found in the gutter outside — her iPhone screen showing thirteen missed calls from my mom, one from Ian, three texts from me, and two from Jovie. My parents didn't seem mad at me, but more like they didn't know what to do with me. They brushed past me in the hallway and would mumble, "Excuse me," but that was it. I didn't know if they blamed me for Kate disappearing or if they hated me because I wasn't a virgin anymore. Or were they simply avoiding me because I reminded them too much of the daughter they feared would never come home.

***

All This Time in the Dark

It has been almost two years since Kate went missing. We celebrated her seventeenth birthday a month after she disappeared, without her. Then we celebrated her eighteenth. She should have graduated from high school. She should have gone to prom. Her bedroom is still the way she left it, pink and shiny like she might come back any day. It's a simple thing, but also not simple at all. She isn't there, but she should be

There was no closure. There was no goodbye. There was no body for us to mourn over. My mom is still convinced that Kate is alive out there somewhere. She says she would be able to feel it if one of her children was no longer alive. But I don't really know if I believe that. Kate always seems, just, *gone* to me. I never think about her coming back.

After Kate went missing, the detective on her case spent every single day at our home for two weeks straight. When nothing turned up except Kate's cell phone right outside, Detective Bristol started coming over less and less. First, it was every other day, then once a week. Now she checks in once a month to remind us that she is doing everything she can. That's usually a phone call, though; she never comes over anymore.

The police questioned Ian and Jovie and Tyler and the entire school. They combed through the neighborhood and tried to find anybody who may have seen where she went that night or, at least, what car she got into. Nobody saw anything. One day, right after she disappeared, I was lying on the couch with my eyes closed. One of the cops came in and pulled Detective Bristol aside, whispering, "It's like she just vanished into thin air." The detective had patted him on the back and shaken her head, but I believed him. Kate was just gone. I didn't think there was an explanation now.

I tried to fight for Kate. I did. But I couldn't keep reliving the night she went missing over and over again. I eventually had to move on with my life. I joined the cheerleading squad in Kate's place. It kept me busy gave me something to think about other than my sister's disappearance. The detective said there might have been a struggle in the driveway and that's why she dropped her phone. It haunts me sometimes, though, because they say the other thing that could have happened was that whoever took her, took her phone away from her and brought it back to the house and dropped it there on purpose. I don't like thinking that the person who took her was right outside of my house twice that night and that I would have been so close to seeing who they were. I hate myself for being sick that night. I hate myself so much.

Ian is gone. After Kate went missing, he went to a different state for college. Some people say he is in Ohio now, but I heard he went to a college in Kansas. Either way, he's long gone. Nobody sees him anymore. Nobody asks about him. He never showed much mercy to any of us for being sad about Kate. He always looked like he knew more than he let on but, whenever I mentioned that to Detective Bristol, she reminded me that they had questioned Ian thoroughly and his story matched that of Tyler's. Ian was at Tyler's party that night and even helped Tyler tap a keg he didn't know how to use. Tyler didn't see Ian around the time Kate would have left the house and gone missing, but it was a crowded party. The police had no need to investigate further into Ian if he had been accounted for that night at Tyler's party, and had even called Kate to try and find out where she was. The missed call and voicemail still sit unanswered on Kate's phone. I didn't believe Ian then — and I still don't — but I have no way to prove that he was lying. Maybe men are just entitled to a life that women don't get to have.

***

Kate is still listed as a missing person, but Detective Bristol said she is now presumed dead. My mom cried at the news. My dad never cried, but sometimes I wished he would, to remind me that he was a little bit human.

They talk about getting divorced now, my mom and dad. They act like they hate each other. My mother drowned her grief in other men; I hear her talking to them on the phone at night when my dad is too drunk to drive home. My father spends his evenings in a bar, drinking away his mistakes. Neither of

All This Time in the Dark

them asks about me much. What's the point in worrying about one daughter when the other one is already gone?

I'm a senior in high school now. Kate would have graduated this past June. They said her name at the graduation ceremony and had her picture sitting on a chair. They showed a slide show of the senior class that ended with her face and everyone cried. I sat in the back of the auditorium and left before anybody could see me or talk to me. I didn't need more sympathetic eyes telling me, "Kate was probably in a better place." No place was a better place if we didn't know where she was. My parents refused to attend the graduation. I didn't blame them — Kate wasn't really there.

My boyfriend, Andrew, would listen to me talk about Kate, but he never asked questions or tilted his head to the side and said stupid shit like, "I'm so sorry they never found her." That's the only reason I started dating him in the first place. He never apologized. I don't know why people apologize when your sister goes missing. It's not like *they* took her. Or maybe they did, I don't know. Detective Bristol always said it was probably someone she knew. Kate wasn't stupid, she wouldn't have just gone off with just anybody, and the detective was convinced I would have heard a fight outside my window if it was some random hobo off the street. I don't really know anymore. It's best if I don't think about it.

They haven't had any leads on Kate in ages. I think maybe they stopped trying, and I don't blame them. A few more kids went missing around here when Kate did, and for a while they had a lead linked to a sex trafficking ring here in Reno, but I never heard of it again and figured it was a dead end. Even with all my searching, I never found her. I never found anything. I would look, hoping I would even find a shoe dropped somewhere on the side of the road, and I never found it. Sometimes, when I was walking through the store, I would examine every woman with dark hair that walked past – hoping it was Kate. But it never was.

So, I moved on with my life. I went out for cheerleading and student council and met Andrew and joined the swim team. I also quit the swim team when I realized I couldn't really swim and was too afraid of getting water up my nose to do the underwater flip to turn around. The coach didn't like me very much. I got good grades and went to average parties on the weekends. I never drank anymore — I was too scared I would end up missing like Kate.

Andrew was good to me and Jovie and I had gotten close after Kate's disappearance. She left for college in Las Vegas, but we still texted every night. Samantha refused to talk to anybody, and I heard she got shipped off to boarding school somewhere after her parents found her cutting her arms up with safety pins, but I don't know if that's true.

We had all moved on and, even though life wasn't the same, it was starting to shine a little brighter than it had the year before. I was getting used to being the only child. I still said I had a sister, but I used to say, "I *have* a sister." When the "have" changes to "had," it usually means things have started to look different.

***

Kate went missing on July 28th, 2017. Detective Bristol called my family on September 4th, 2019.

I answered the phone.

"Hello?" I said. I don't know why we still had a home telephone since we all just used our cell phones for everything anyways.

"This is Detective Bristol. Am I speaking with Haddie?"

"Oh. Hi. Yeah, it's Haddie."

"Haddie, are your parents' home?"

"My mom is, do you want me to get her?" She usually just called to check-in every few weeks. We stopped getting excited to hear from her months ago.

"Yes, please."

All This Time in the Dark

"Mom!" I shouted while holding the phone away from my face, "The detective wants to talk to you!"

"Just come in the room and get me, Haddie, there's no need to shout."

I rolled my eyes and handed her the phone. "Hello?" she said.

I sat down on the bar stool in our bright, white kitchen and spun around a few times. I glanced at my Mom as she talked on the phone. Her face turned red, then went completely white. Her hand flew to her mouth as she turned towards the sink and puked.

"Mom! Gross! What's wrong?" My stomach dropped and I figured the worst: Kate was dead. She had to be. My mom wouldn't react that way if the detective was just calling to "check-in."

"Mrs. Anderson?" I heard Detective Bristol from the phone sitting on the counter.

My mom splashed water on her face and burst into tears.

I picked up the phone, "My mom isn't feeling so well."

"Haddie, we found Kate."

"Is she dead?"

"No, she's alive."

"She's alive?! You found her, and she's alive?!"

"She's alive, Haddie, your sister, is coming home to you."

I burst into tears and raced over to hug my mom. I didn't understand what that meant, or what anybody was saying, but, damn, it sounded so good.

My mom kissed my forehead and grabbed the phone. "Where do we go? What do we do?"

She nodded a few times and hung up. "I need to call your father. We have to fly to Las Vegas tonight."

***

I packed my bags in a rush, knowing that, in two hours, we would be with my sister. Our flight left in forty-five minutes. It seemed like an eternity away. I shoved clothes in my suitcase and then went into Kate's room and threw some of her favorite clothes into a small bag for her. I didn't know if she'd need them. I didn't know where she had been.

The flight to Vegas, while only forty-five minutes seemed like it took a year. I couldn't stop fidgeting. Even though my parents hated each other, they held hands the entire time. My mom couldn't stop crying. My dad sat completely still like he was made of stone.

Detective Bristol met us at the airport. She was a strong, beautiful woman, six feet tall, but not overweight. She wore her dark, curly hair around her face. I hugged her when I saw her; I wasn't sure why.

We piled into an unmarked SUV, which I figured was a cop car, but didn't ask.

The detective started off by saying, "She's not herself. She hasn't had the best few years."

"What does that mean?" my mom asked.

"A detective down here in Vegas traced a man named Mike and followed him for a long time. He was a suspect in a sex trafficking ring. It took a long time to find out where he was working and what he was doing. He had a regular house in the Las Vegas suburbs. An undercover cop finally got an appointment with one of Mike's girls. Once Mike asked for money, the officer arrested him. When they searched the house, they found six girls working there and Kate was one of them. They traced Mike to two other houses and multiple motels between here and Reno. We found twenty-eight girls. A few of them refused to come with us. Unfortunately, three women were found dead in motel rooms. We aren't sure how many more he has, or how many others have died in his care."

My dad's face turned red and my Mom burst into tears.

"I don't understand," I finally said. "Sex trafficking? Like Kate was being used as a sex slave? Or like this Mike guy was forcing her to have sex with him?"

All This Time in the Dark

"Well, it sounds like she was being forced to have sex with a lot of other men so Mike could get money. He was selling her."

"I thought sex trafficking was something in Europe like in that movie, *Taken*."

"Unfortunately, it happens everywhere. It's big money for these kinds of people."

"Did you say the man who took her was named Mike?" I asked.

"We aren't sure if he was the one who actually took her, but he was the one in charge."

"Ian had a brother named Mike," I said.

"What?" my mother asked.

"Mike was Ian's brother's name. One night, Kate and I snuck out to Ian's house, and Mike was there. Ian said, 'Watch out for my brother,' and he seemed nervous and scared. We left, but Kate said she saw Mike watching her from the window of Ian's house, and it scared her. She promised me she wouldn't go back to their house again but, I don't know, maybe she did."

"We'll definitely look into that, Haddie."

"Where is Mike now?"

"In jail."

"Oh."

"We're hoping he doesn't get out for a long time."

"Oh."

"Look, I need to be honest with you all. This isn't the same Kate you knew when she left that night. She looks a lot different. She's been through a lot and you might not recognize her. I will warn you, she is bruised. The hospital found a few broken ribs and a broken arm that hadn't properly healed, and she has a few other conditions I'll let her tell you about."

We pulled up to the hospital, and all three of us raced out of the car. Detective Bristol had warned us not to rush her, that she was jumpy, but I didn't really care. She was my sister and my best friend, and I was going to see her *now*.

We rounded the corner to the floor the nurses said she was on. The detective got stuck in the lobby, talking to another family. Twenty-eight girls were found, that was twenty-eight families they needed to find.

As we pushed open the door to her room, I saw the hills her feet made under the white hospital blanket. The TV was on and her head was turned to the side to see it. Her face was bandaged in some spots, she had a black eye and tape across her nose. I wondered if they'd had to fix that. She was so, so pale, her skin looked like it might peel off of her. I scanned the rest of her body, the skinny arms hanging at her sides, covered in dark circles. I figured her legs looked the same, like she had been hit over and over again. Her full head of hair was now stringy with circular patches of scalp showing through. The only part that looked like it'd had any food at all was her perfectly round stomach poking out from under the blankets.

"KATE!" my mother screamed as she rushed towards her.

Kate's eyes widened and she shrank away from my mother's embrace before realizing who it was. When her eyes met mine, she started to cry.

"I never thought I'd see you again," she said. Her voice sounded hoarse, not like hers. "They killed Angel and sold Candy, and I thought they were going to kill me, too," she cried out. She was sobbing in my mother's arms, but her arms had dropped back to the bed like they were too heavy to hold up.

My father looked uncomfortable and walked out of the room.

A doctor in bright red scrubs and a white lab coat came into the room. Her pale hair was piled high on top of her head and she wore a pin on her shirt that said *Let me know how I can help!* with a smiley face.

"The family is here!" she said brightly. Like we didn't know who we were. Like we should be excited to see my sister half-dead in a hospital bed.

All This Time in the Dark

They never showed this part in movies — the aftermath, I mean. The people are always excited to see each other and the missing person just has a scrape or two. But it was never this bad. It was never this dark.

"Well, Miss Kate is healing quite well! Since she came in early this morning, she's perked up quite a bit. Her blood pressure is stable. We'll have to take her into surgery a bit later to fix her arm, nose, and ribs, but it looks like she and the baby are going to be okay."

We all froze, and our eyes flashed first to Kate, then to her stomach, then to the doctor in her bright white lab coat. "The what?" my mother asked.

"You didn't know," the doctor said. Her smile faded, and she slowly started to back out of the room, "I'll give you guys a minute."

I watched her back out of the room and noticed that my father had been standing in the doorway. He looked sick. I had never seen him look so old and worn before. I had never noticed his dark black hair graying by his temples or the dark circles pasted under his eyes. Maybe that was new. Or, maybe, that was the shock from the thought of his teenage daughter fucking a dude and getting pregnant.

"Kate, I…" my mom started, then she froze and just sat down on Kate's bed.

Kate absently placed a hand on her stomach. It looked round but not as round as my aunt did when she was pregnant with my cousin. "I don't even know what to say," Kate said.

"Is it true?" my mother asked.

"I guess, yeah. I'm pregnant."

"Who's the father?" my dad said. Even I could tell that was a question Kate was never going to be able to answer.

Kate looked suddenly angry. Like she couldn't believe anybody would ever question her on anything. Her eyes darkened, and she looked like she wanted to kill someone, "I don't fucking know, Father. I would assume it was one of the guys who fucked me, but I've been fucking five guys a day for over a year, so there's like eighteen hundred choices of men out there. Good luck finding him."

"Kate!" my mother gasped.

"Oh, sis," I said.

"Well, that's a really stupid question! They told you where I was, right?"

"Just in a house," I answered.

"It wasn't a house. It was hell. It was a place where they sell your body for pennies all for a few good minutes for some guy."

I noticed that she was shaking slightly. "Are you okay?" I asked her.

"It's the withdrawal," she said, and her face reddened slightly. I noticed she looked embarrassed.

My head reeled. Eighteen hundred different guys had fucked my sister. How would any of us ever move past this? How could Kate survive this? This wasn't Kate, this woman sitting in front of me. She looked like the homeless women I passed on the street when my parents took us to San Francisco for my ninth birthday. One of them, who couldn't have been more than twenty, was sitting in the rain with half an umbrella. Her eyes looked old and worn. I wanted to buy her an umbrella so badly. I figured everybody deserved the chance to stay dry. Wasn't that a human right? But we came out of the store she was sitting in front of, she was gone. I never knew what happened to her, but her umbrella half was sitting on the sidewalk where she had been, so I always hoped she had gotten a new one. I had never really seen homeless people until then. I didn't know what they looked like, except for the few I saw in movies. Looking at Kate now, she reminded me so much of the woman with half an umbrella, it broke my heart.

My mom sighed and left the room in search of the doctor. My father turned around to follow her, leaving Kate and me alone, facing each other.

All This Time in the Dark

I tentatively sat on the edge of her bed and then popped back up. Sitting on her bed was something I would have done before she left that night. I didn't know if I still had that right anymore.

Kate laughed, "You can sit there."

"I didn't know if I should."

"You look older," she said.

"I guess I am, but I don't usually feel it."

"I feel old and exhausted. There's a world out there I didn't know existed, and I don't think I will ever feel young again."

My eyes filled with tears. "I thought about you every day. If I hadn't been sick that night, I could have gone with you. I could have stopped this."

"Oh, Haddie. I never blamed you, you know that? I never blamed you for even a second. This wasn't your fault. Okay?"

I shrugged, "I still blame myself."

"I blame myself, too," she said.

"It wasn't your fault."

"It was. I trusted Ian when everyone told me not to."

"Did he do this to you?"

"Not really, but he took me to Mike and left me there. He knows what he did."

"He's gone now, you know."

"Where?"

"College, I guess, but now I'm wondering if that's true."

"I doubt he's in college now. I hope he's in jail."

"Kate, there's so much I want to ask you…" I glanced up at her, and she didn't look mad like she had at my dad. Maybe she blamed my parents for not protecting her. Maybe she still felt about me the way I felt about her. Maybe we were still best friends after all of this.

"You can ask me anything," she said, but she looked sad. She didn't really want to talk to me about it, I could tell.

"I just want to know what happened. I can't make any sense out of this."

"Oh, Haddie. I used to be jealous of you. Did you know that? Samantha and I used to listen in on your phone calls, back before I met Ian. We used to hear you talk about your boyfriends, and you were always so pretty and confident. I used to wish I could be like that."

"I never knew that."

"I was your older sister, Haddie, I couldn't tell you that to your face," we both laughed, "but it's true."

"I missed you so much, Kate."

"Nothing will ever be the same."

I looked down at my hands, "I know."

"I don't want this baby," she said, rubbing her belly, "I don't want anything to do with it. I told the doctor I wanted to put it up for adoption. She told me to think about it, but I don't want to think about it. Every time it kicks me, I wish I was dead. I can't do it, Haddie. I can't be a mother to a child who was made this way. A child who was made from rape. That's what it was, you know. Mike can say whatever he wants, but none of us ever wanted it from those guys. Most of them were fat and gross and old, and I always just closed my eyes and hoped it would end. Most of the time it hurt. I couldn't do anything about it, Haddie. I couldn't stop it. I couldn't leave. One of the girls I shared a room was killed while I hid in the bathroom. God, Haddie, I heard her head being stomped into the ground as she died. I sat by her as she bled out from her skull. I saw it, Haddie, I saw everything, and I couldn't stop it." Kate was crying by the time she was done, but I didn't think she knew that she was. The tears just rolled absently down her face and made the bandage on her nose wet around the edges. She looked so sad, but so old all at the same time. The only part that still looked like Kate was her smile, but she wasn't using it.

"Some of the other girls said they shot girls in front of them," she continued, "I watched as one of the girls got taken out of her room and sold to a different man because she was about to have a baby. I watched her kick and scream and beg not to go. I wish I could find her now, Haddie. I wish I could find all those girls and hold on to them so tightly. I wish there was some way I could fix the evil in the world. I wish I could stop it, even if it was just for a few moments. I don't understand it, I really don't. I don't understand why people do bad things and why people hurt other people. I sat there for a year and wondered how a man could force a woman to be someone he wanted her to be, and we just had to sit there and take it and take it and take it."

I leaned forward to wipe the tears from her eyes, but she pulled back, not rudely, but like she couldn't stand the thought of being touched. "Kate, I don't know how to fix this for you."

"You're sitting in front of me, Haddie, that's all I need right now. You aren't asking me those stupid questions and poking me and prodding me. You aren't questioning me for information on Mike or looking at me like I'm insane for not wanting this baby."

"I wouldn't want the baby either," I shrugged. I got it.

"I've been addicted to heroin and cocaine. They gave it to me because I was so depressed about the baby. It numbed the pain for the last month. The doctor said I was going through withdrawals from it. They didn't say it like I was a drug addict or a bad person. They felt *bad* for me. Like they wanted to help me. *Like they pitied me."*

"God, Kate, I don't even know."

"They said they're worried about the damage to the baby. I don't know anymore, Haddie, I just don't. I don't know if we can tell what will be wrong with her until she's born."

I reached for her hand and, this time, she didn't pull away. She just looked down at my hand as though love and affection were the weirdest things she had ever seen in her life.

***

I snuck out of Kate's room once she had fallen asleep. My parents were nowhere to be found; I assumed they were either somewhere fighting or calling everyone they knew. Either way, I didn't want to be a part of it.

I wandered towards the cafeteria. Detective Bristol was sitting at a table there, drinking coffee and staring off into space. I sat down across from her, and she smiled when she saw me. "Hi, Haddie."

"Detective," I nodded.

"You can call me Rachel."

"Rachel, I guess."

"How is Kate doing?" she asked me.

"Kate isn't Kate anymore."

"I'm sorry."

"Do you ever think you should have done more? Like, maybe, you could have found her sooner?"

The detective looked sad when I asked. She sighed and stared at her hands for a while. I almost got up, sure that she wasn't going to answer me at all, but she finally looked up and caught my gaze. She looked at me like that for a long time and then said, "I have to be honest. The first time I got called to your house, I assumed Kate had run away. I even questioned your dad repeatedly, looking for signs of familial strife. I'm not proud of myself but, in my line of work, when a teenage girl goes missing, it's usually because she chose to run off with some boyfriend or got into drugs. After I talked to you, Haddie, I was almost sure she had run away to do drugs with some of the people you had been hanging out with that summer. It makes me sound like a bad person, but it is what it is. I see it all the time. The good girl has one drink or does one line of cocaine and, all of a sudden, their world shifts. They realize how much they missed out on by being good in school and they move down a dangerous road."

All This Time in the Dark

I stared at her, but she didn't continue right away. She took a drink of her coffee and set it back down, staring at the cup. "But she didn't run away. You know that now."

Rachel looked back up at me and I saw a tear roll down her cheek. "Sometimes this job is just so damn impossible, Haddie. I mean, I reported her as missing, but my colleagues and I thought we knew better. We figured we'd find her somewhere, like San Francisco, which is a close enough drive from Reno but far enough away for her to get lost in the drug scene. It's pretty easy, once you're in it, to never get out. Maybe I judge too much, or maybe I judge too quickly. Whatever I have done, I guess, isn't the problem here. I feel like I owe your entire family an apology."

"So, you could have done more." It wasn't a question.

"It's so much more complicated than that, Haddie. There's a protocol to follow. There are steps I have to take. Even if I thought Ian *had* done it, I couldn't do anything about it without some sort of reason. My hands are tied by this job. I can only do so much."

"Maybe someone should do something about that."

She looked back down at her hands. "Maybe they should," she mumbled.

We sat in silence for a long time before Rachel asked, "Aren't you glad we found her at least?"

"I'm glad she's back. I don't think she's alive though."

"You see it in her eyes, too, don't you?"

"She's not the same," I answered.

"When they first found her, she was drugged out of her mind. She couldn't even lift her head up. She couldn't respond to her name and just kept saying, 'Call me Daisey,' over and over and over again. When a male officer tried to get her out of the room and take her to the hospital, she laid down on the bed, spread her legs, and pulled her nightgown up."

"Fuck," I whispered.

"She was emaciated to the point of discomfort when we found her. Everything about her looked like it had sunken in. I compared her face to the face of the girl in the picture your parents had handed me on night one, and I could barely make a connection. Where she had once been soft, sweet, and innocent, she now looked hard, with cheekbones that jutted out from her face. Her collarbone showed so much it made me hurt to look at it. She could barely stand on her legs. If it helps, Haddie, the other girls weren't in any better shape, though. The stretch of land between Reno and Las Vegas is endless waves of nothing but empty desert. The road stretches through mid-Nevada with nothing to see except dirt, a few small desert plants, and occasionally a small animal running across the road — the loneliest highway on the planet. But, littered between stretches of dirt are small, long-forgotten towns nobody thinks about except the people who live there and love it there. Tonopah, Mina, Luning, Hawthorne, Goldfield, Beatty; all dot the lonely land out west.

"It's a beautiful desert with unlimited amounts of history. But it's also forgotten, and the small motels along the way are perfect if you want to find yourself ignored and left alone. In that way, Mike ran the perfect operation. He gave a cut of his profits to the motel managers. They turned the other way, and no one was the wiser. Unlike some operations we had discovered, Mike's was more upscale. And, even though his girls were almost dead, they were still better off than some of the girls and boys we find."

"It doesn't mean Kate is okay."

"I know it doesn't," Detective Bristol continued. Her eyes looked broken. She looked so much older today than she did when I first met her. "It's just that two of the girls we rescued were starved to the point of delusion. One of them was so strung up on cocaine, she still hasn't been able to tell us her real name. We can't find a missing person case open on anyone who resembles her, so she may have gone completely unnoticed off into the depths of Mike's soul. Kate, on the other hand, spent hours telling us she was Daisey. And another hour after that, crying because she was scared Mike would hear her telling us her real name. By the time we got it out of her, we had matched her description with Kate's missing person case anyways, and you and your parents were already on your way. There's a connection you two have. One that only sisters understand. That's all I mean about Kate. I think she'll be okay. She isn't alone in this world."

"Kate told me things — things I didn't even know existed in this world. The bad parts of the world nobody wants to go down like a never-ending rabbit hole of pain. I just nodded like everything she was saying was the most normal thing in the world, but I'm scared, Detective, I'm so scared." I noticed that, when I looked into her eyes, she refused to meet mine.

Detective Bristol nodded as her phone vibrated loudly against the table. She glanced at it and hit the decline call button, but also took one last drink of coffee and stood up to go. She had to work; I knew that. "You know, Haddie, tomorrow they're going to send in psychologists and doctors to analyze her. They're going to try and make sense of what's happened to her, and they're going to try to get her to make sense of it, too. We're human. It's how we cope with things. If someone can make sense of what happened to Kate, then maybe it won't happen to them. Or, if people standing on the outside can judge what happened to Kate, then they'll be above it. Now that she's here, the reporters and journalists and magazines and newspapers will all show up and want to know every last detail. She'll be the girl who was found — they all will. And everyone in the world will analyze what happened to her, because if they can find some misstep she took, or some fault to pin on me, then they will sleep better at night knowing they would never be that stupid. But these things could happen to anyone. They could even happen to me. Nobody is exempt from pain or heartache. We all know that we just try to justify it away and hope it never comes around again."

I stood up to face her. "But don't you think someone has a quota of pain in their lives? Like if something really bad happens, don't you think that it will be over for them, then? That now, nothing bad will happen to Kate ever again, because she's already suffered enough?"

Detective Bristol laughed, "I wish I knew the answer to that, Haddie." She paused and glanced down at the phone in her hand, which was ringing again. She declined the call and returned her attention to me. "I was raped once, you know? When I was thirteen. Someone I thought I trusted came into my room one night and turned into someone I didn't know. It made me want to do what I do for a living. I wanted to get revenge on guys like him. I've learned that it doesn't really work that way, though. There's never any satisfaction, and there is no such thing as saving the world. Nobody believed me. Nobody believed I had been raped. They all told me I had asked for it because he was my older brother's friend. I wish I could tell you what that felt like and what that did to me. But I guess it's just another way people wish away the evils of the world."

"So, what do I say to her? To Kate, I mean. What would you have wanted someone to say to you?"

"That you believed me. That you were sorry for me. That his sorry ass deserved to be in jail for a long, long time. But, also, maybe just listening is good, too. Maybe sometimes there's nothing to say. Maybe people just can't be healed right away, even if it makes everyone else uncomfortable. We all want so badly to rush through heartache and pain because it's uncomfortable, but sometimes people just can't be healed right away, and that's probably okay."

I smiled at her and nodded because I didn't know what else to say. She hugged me and walked off down the hallway, picking up her phone as she did.

"Detective Bristol here," I heard her say, "I have to give my two weeks' notice. I'm leaving the force."

Maybe everything just got to be too much for her, too.

***

All This Time in the Dark

"What do we do?" I heard my mom ask my dad later that night. They thought I was asleep. Kate and I were curled up together on her bed, but I don't think Kate was really asleep either. They just thought we were.

"I don't know."

"I can't believe this is happening." I heard my mom start crying again.

"She's too young to be a mother," my dad whispered.

"There are options," my mom whispered back.

"Like what? It's not like there's a father we can call."

"She can give it up for adoption."

"Adoption? Jessica, I just don't know if she can do that. It's still her baby."

"But it isn't really, is it, Robert? Will it feel like her baby when she looks down at it and remembers every single day how it was conceived? There are so many families out there who could love it."

"I don't think she can just give away her baby."

"All it will be is a reminder for her." My mom sounded like she was begging, but I didn't know what for. It wasn't *their* baby.

"I don't think that's a decision I'm going to allow."

"Well, I'm sorry to say, it isn't your decision to make. Kate is eighteen now. She can do whatever she wants with her body and her baby, Robert. Men like you don't have a right to tell a woman what she can and cannot do with her body."

My dad didn't say anything. He cleared his throat and sat there for a while and then I heard him whisper, "Excuse me," and his footsteps took him out of the room. I opened my eyes and looked towards my mom. She was perched on the edge of the hospital chair, glancing up at the television glowing in the corner of the room. Her face was illuminated by the glow of the screen and she looked even older.

"Mom?" I whispered.

She turned to look at me, and a tear rolled down her cheek, "Did we wake you up?"

"No, I was awake."

"You heard us?"

"I did."

"I'm sorry."

"It's not your fault, Mom."

"I couldn't save her from this," my mom said.

"None of us could have."

"It's my job to save her from stuff like this. I'm her mother. It's my job to protect her."

I didn't say anything. I wasn't a mother; I had no right to say what a parent should or should not do. Nobody who isn't a parent knows what it's actually like to be one.

"I never want to have kids," I finally told her.

"You might change your mind one day, Haddie. I used to say the same thing."

"What made you change your mind?"

She laughed softly, "Kate was a big surprise. I guess I didn't have a choice."

"For what it's worth, I think you protected us both the best you could." She smiled. "Thanks, Haddie."

"What if Kate keeps the baby?"

"Then we figure it out."

"Mom?"

"Yeah, Haddie?"

"Kate told me she didn't want to keep it."

"I know, hon, she told me that, too. I think she's making the right decision by finding a good family for it."

"Mom?"

"Yeah, Haddie?"

"I'm sorry if I ever let you down."

I noticed tears rolling down her cheeks again. She looked away from me and wiped her face. She always refused to cry in front of me and Kate, but I never knew why. When she cried in front of me, it just reminded me that she was human, too. It made her more relatable.

"Haddie, you and Kate could never, ever let me down."

"I love you, Mom."

***

When Kate finally came home six days later, she walked around the house like a zombie. She waddled slightly now because of the baby and she didn't look anything like her old self. She looked older and worn. She was exhausted all of the time. The doctor said that was because of the baby, too, but when we were alone, she would tell me she just couldn't sleep at night. I don't know if she ever slept. I always saw her just staring at the ceiling, lying there, not moving. Like she was afraid if she started to move, everything would break.

I missed the old Kate. I even missed the way we fought. And, after six full days of talking about nothing but Kate and hearing my parents fight about Kate and listening to the detectives' questioning Kate, and having psychologists pour over Kate, I was so over the entire thing, I just wanted to go to bed. It's not that I didn't have sympathy for what Kate had been through, I did, but I mattered, too, and not once had anybody asked if I was okay.

The doctors in Las Vegas hadn't wanted Kate to fly home so we had to drive. They didn't want her to leave the hospital at all since she was about to give birth in the next few weeks — and they didn't know what condition that baby would be in — but my father had "put his foot down" and demanded that Kate get back to normal. Even though normal didn't exist right now and probably wouldn't for a while.

Tessa M. Osborne

As soon as we got home, Jovie burst through the door. She was home for the summer from college, and I had called her when they said they'd found Kate.

"You're BACK!" she screamed and ran to hug Kate. Kate shrunk back like she always did now when anybody tried to love her.

"Jovie," Kate said. She had this weird way of talking now. Like she was a robot. Or half dead. Every now and then, when it was just the two of us, she would come alive, like a switch had been flipped, and then she would start talking about where she had been. She ran her sentences together, like her thoughts couldn't come out fast enough. But, most of the time, she just responded when people said things like there was no connection between her mind and her mouth anymore.

"I was so worried about you! I can't believe you're alive!"

"Me, neither."

"Tell me all about it. I can't believe you're PREGNANT! OH MY GOD!"

"Yeah."

"How do you feel? Is it a boy or a girl?"

"Fine. I don't know."

Jovie sat down on our couch and pulled Kate's hand so Kate would sit down next to her. Kate perched on the edge of the couch like it was made of knives and crossed her hands over her stomach.

"I just can't believe this, Kate! I never thought you would come home!" Jovie started to cry.

Kate glanced at me, standing by the wall like a creep, and shrugged her shoulders. I smiled at her and shrugged back.

"I mean," Jovie sobbed, "I thought you were dead and gone forever."

"I wish I was," Kate said, and Jovie and I didn't know what to say.

***

All This Time in the Dark

Long after Jovie left, when the house was quiet for the night, I crept into Kate's room. I thought I would find her asleep, but she was wide awake, just lying on her bed, on top of the covers, staring at the ceiling. I don't know if my parents noticed that she did this. I think they were too excited to have her home; they didn't notice that she wasn't even close to Kate. She just kind of looked like her.

"Can I come in?" I said to the dark outline of her body lying on the bed.

"Sure," she said. Her head lolled to the side to acknowledge me and then turned back to the ceiling.

"You doing okay?"

"I guess."

"You want to talk about anything?"

"Not really."

I sat on the edge of her bed and she reached her hand down towards me. I brushed the hair from of her eyes and her face was wet with tears. I grabbed the hand reaching out for me and held it tight.

"I wish I had died back there, Haddie. I wish I hadn't made it home. I want to crawl out of my skin. Nobody here understands, nobody gets it. They don't show you this part in the movies, you know? When the girl comes home and finally makes it back, and nothing feels right. Everything is wrong, and off, and I feel so… antsy… yet tired all at the same time."

"I don't know what to say, Kate. I'm so sorry."

"I feel the baby kick sometimes and I wish it wouldn't. I just want it out of me. It's a constant reminder."

"Dad thinks you're going to keep it."

"Dad can kiss my ass."

"Him and mom are going to get a divorce," I say.

Her eyes turn towards me, and she sits up in bed, the way she always used to when we were talking late at night, and she would get excited about something, "What? Tell me!"

I laughed because I had missed this and hadn't realized just how much. "They fight all the time. I heard them one night say they were waiting for me to graduate, and then they were going to call it quits. I told Mom the next day they should just do it now, so I didn't have to live with their fighting any longer."

Kate's eyes flashed in front of me like an entire world just ran through her mind. I didn't know where to go from here, I didn't know what to say. I wanted so badly to just move on and forget that anything had ever happened, but Kate seemed so stuck.

"I wish I could have been here for that."

I shrugged, "I guess you're here now, right?"

"Am I, though?"

"I don't really know anymore."

***

Kate went into labor at 3:52 am, almost one month exactly since she had been home. She woke me up, screaming for my mother because her water had broken all over her bed. It wasn't a cute trickle like it was in the movies — it was like a goddamn lake flooded her mattress. She was screaming and panicked and kept saying, "Just get it out," over and over again.

I followed them to the hospital in my own car. I didn't want to go at all, but Kate had asked me to be there for her. I couldn't say no. Wasn't the baby technically my niece or nephew anyways? Is that how it worked?

Kate had an adoption agency and a family waiting for the baby. I don't think she wanted it any other way. She was only in labor for five hours before it was time for her to push. The epidural had kept her mostly out of pain. I held

All This Time in the Dark

her hand while she pushed and our mother held the other. The three of us cried when the baby girl was finally born.

It was the most disgusting but beautiful thing I had ever seen. I was thoroughly disgusted and made a hasty decision to never, ever, have children. The amount of blood all over the room and the bed looked like a horror scene, but they kept saying everything looked good. She only had to push five times — five times and the baby was born. They kept yelling at her to push like she was pooping and, when I laughed, the nurse gave me a dirty look. I guess it worked, though, because the baby slid out so easily. Kate was sweating and cursing and shaking the entire time. I don't think she ever stopped crying.

They tried to hand her to Kate, but Kate refused to hold her. She wouldn't even look at her. When the baby was born, Kate turned to look at me, then shut her eyes as tight as she could. She cried while holding my hand so tightly I thought it would break. I kissed the top of her head and brushed the hair out of her eyes.

"Are you sure," the nurse asked, "that you don't want to hold her?"

Kate didn't say a word, just quietly shook her head no. Her eyes shut tight. My mother held her other hand and leaned down and whispered something in her ear I couldn't quite make out. Kate nodded and leaned her head into my mother's chest and sobbed. I didn't realize someone could cry so hard without falling all the way apart.

The nurse took the baby to a room next door and I was later told the adoptive family had been waiting there. They had to stay at the hospital for a night and take the baby home in 24 hours. They stitched Kate up and left her in recovery. My mother went out to call my father. I sat on the couch next to her bed; the one I assumed was there for excited fathers-to-be. The nurse kept telling me it pulled out, and I could lie down, but I didn't think I should.

"It's over," Kate whispered to me when the room was empty. She hadn't moved much yet and, when she did that, I could tell she felt weird. She said her legs were waking up and felt tingly. She said it felt like when you have a cavity filled, and your mouth is numb, but then a few hours later, it starts to wake up, and it feels like little pinpricks everywhere. I guess I understood that.

"It's over," I repeated.

"Did you see her?" she asked me.

"Yeah, I did."

"Was she okay?"

"Aw, Kate, she was beautiful. Dark blue eyes and bright blonde hair. She looked like your baby pictures."

Kate smiled. "I was scared there would be something wrong with her."

"Because of everything?"

"Because of the drugs."

"Yeah, I wondered that, too."

"But she was really okay?"

"She looked perfect to me." I didn't know if the baby was okay, really, but it wasn't our baby anymore. It wasn't up to me to know.

Kate smiled again. "Good."

"Are you sure you don't want to see her?"

"She isn't mine, Haddie. She was never mine."

I looked out the window. Outside, the world looked so normal. The sun was shining and I could see people walking to work. One lady was on her phone. She threw her head back and laughed. I wanted, so badly, to walk outside and be one of them. I thought if I could just walk outside and stand on the street corner and laugh like that, maybe some of this would make sense. Maybe I could wrap my head around it.

"I wish I could help you, Kate."

Kate smirked and looked up at me. "I just needed her to be born."

I nodded. I didn't know what that meant. I didn't know what to say back. Maybe Kate just needed her out so she could heal and truly be over what happened. Maybe, just maybe, we could all just get back to normal.

All This Time in the Dark

***

Kate had to spend forty-eight hours in the hospital. They said it was so she could heal and see a few counselors that would "verify" her mental health after the adoption, but I don't know how true that was. She only saw a counselor twice, and both times they asked her a list of ten questions and then left.

"How are you doing?"

"Fine."

"Do you have any thoughts of hurting yourself or someone else?"

"No."

"Do you feel like you made the right decision?"

"Yes."

"Do you have any regrets or feelings you want to talk about?"

"No."

"Do you want to meet your daughter?"

"She isn't my daughter."

"Do you want to know anything about the adoptive family?"

"No."

"Do you have a solid, stable place to go home to to heal?"

"Yes, my parents' house."

"How do you feel physically?"

"Like I just had a baby."

"Do you need anything else?"

"No, thank you."

Then they would hand her a business card and tell her to call if she needed anything. They couldn't have been there more than twenty minutes. The nurse who came in after they left said that it was just "standard protocol." She asked Kate how she was feeling, and then she left, too. Nobody seemed that interested in the answer.

Kate slept most of the time in the hospital. I tried to leave one day, but her eyes snapped open and she begged me to stay with her. She said she didn't like the white of the hospital walls, she just couldn't be alone. I slept on the little pull-out couch. Babies cried in the hallway at night. I stayed awake late and watched *Teen Mom* re-runs on the TV.

They discharged Kate on a Wednesday afternoon. When we stepped outside to leave, the sun was shining.

"I think things will get better," I said to Kate.

"I just needed her to be born," Kate repeated again.

***

Life is a very weird thing, so finite and fragile. If I could just grasp on to my own life, maybe I could make sense of something. But, since Kate disappeared so long ago, I haven't been able to make sense of much of anything. For too long now, I felt like I was living in someone else's life. I desperately wanted to grasp on to what I thought my life *was,* but, sometimes, I think that maybe what my life was and what my life is will never be the same.

Maybe Kate felt that way, too.

I didn't leave the house much anymore. Nobody ever wanted to leave Kate, and I never wanted to be away from her. But sometimes we needed to go live our lives, also. Cheerleading was still a part of me, and I couldn't let that go. My mother, and the counselor she had hired, said I needed to live as normal a life as possible. I guessed that was true, but I didn't know what was normal anymore. I wished I did.

Kate came home from the hospital on Wednesday. My mother and father went back to work on Thursday. I left the house for two hours on Thursday afternoon to catch a quick cheer practice before I spent the rest of the night in my sister's room. I promised her we could start watching all the movies she hadn't been able to see when she was "gone."

That was how I put it to her: "When you were gone." She had a funny look on her face when I said it, but she didn't stop me or correct me. Her eyes never really looked like they came back, so maybe she was still gone. But I had

All This Time in the Dark

kept a list of all the movies I saw when she was gone, and I wanted to show them to her. I wanted to give her a reason to come back to us.

I was excited that day after cheer. I thought the world would go back and keep spinning, and normal wasn't too far away. The sun was out. As I walked to my car, I threw my head back and laughed. It felt incredible. It felt the way it used to.

Kate had only been alone at the house for two hours. I left at noon and was pulling into the driveway at 1:57 pm. I unlocked the front door and noticed how quiet it was. It was so damn quiet. Kate wasn't watching TV. Even the fridge wasn't making the hum it sometimes does when it makes ice. The curtains and windows were closed. It was dark and just so damn quiet.

"Kate?" I yelled into the empty room.

She didn't answer, so I went to her room to see if she was asleep. Her bed was perfectly made, and there was a small note sitting on top of her pink pillow. It was folded into a cootie catcher like we used to make at school. I could never make them. I used to come home at night and cry because all the other girls could fold the paper the right way to make it work, and I never could. Kate would roll her eyes and fold the paper for me to take to school the next day.

I picked up the cootie catcher and bounced it between my hands. She must have been playing around. I laughed, "Good call, Kate, now we can find out who we're going to marry. Pick a number."

I moved it between my fingers and counted to thirteen. Kate's favorite number was always thirteen I walked down the hallway to the bathroom. The door was shut, but the water wasn't running, so she was probably just going to the bathroom.

"Kate, you okay?" It took her longer in the bathroom these days — more cleanup after the baby, I suppose — but she at least always answered.

"Kate?"

She still didn't answer.

Tessa M. Osborne

I banged on the door. I tried the door handle, and it twisted in my hand.

I realized a part of me didn't want to open the door. *She just needed to be born,* Kate had been saying over and over. I thought that meant she needed it to be over so she could live her life. But, as I stood outside the closed bathroom door, I wondered if it was something different.

I wondered if Kate felt the finality of life, the same way I did. I wondered if she felt that, one day, everything could collapse in on us. I wondered if she felt like it already had.

Kate had been used and battered and beaten, and she was stuck somewhere in her head. Somewhere, in her mind, she just couldn't leave Mike and what he had done to her. Or what had been done to her by other people. She didn't have the help she needed. Once she was found safe, nobody questioned her sanity. Everyone just assumed she would be so happy to get home, but I didn't know if she was.

Somewhere along the way, I knew Kate had made a choice that no matter what, her life wasn't worth living anymore.

I pushed the bathroom door open just a crack. "Kate?" I whispered.

I glanced into the room, not wanting to see, not wanting to know. I was still grasping the cootie catcher, the paper turning wet from the sweat on my hands.

"Kate?" I whispered again.

And then I saw her, my beautiful sister, draped in the bathtub. Her hair was flung over the edge. Her eyes were closed, and her lips were slightly parted. They were pale, but her cheeks still looked flushed. Like she was warm. Or the way they looked when she got embarrassed. She looked like she was sleeping; her face was so peaceful.

It wasn't until I crept closer that I saw the blood in the bathtub. It looked like so much blood, but then I realized she wasn't wearing any clothes, and the bathtub was full of water. *What are you doing in the bathtub, Kate? You aren't moving, Kate. Start moving!* I touched her shoulder and her skin felt so warm. She had to just be asleep.

"Kate, wake up," I said, shaking her shoulder. I didn't understand why she would fall asleep in the bathtub. *Where is the blood coming from?*

"KATE!" I yelled, shaking her harder.

When I shook her, I heard the quiet clank of something bouncing between her body and the side of the bathtub. It sounded medal.

Why won't she move?

My foot kicked something plastic as I stood up to back away from the bathtub. I bent over and picked up my father's blood thinner medication. The bottle was empty. It was just refilled two days ago and had been full. Now it was empty, and I was holding it in my hand trying to figure out what that meant. Trying to decide if Kate was going to live or die.

"Kate, no. No, no, no, no, no. Kate, what did you do? Kate, how could you do this? Kate, please wake up, please wake up."

I fell to the ground, shaking and sobbing. I couldn't catch my breath. *Why is all the oxygen leaving this house? Why is this room so out of air?* I thought. But then I realized I was screaming.

I ran out of the house, the cootie catcher still in my hand. I forgot my phone, but I didn't want to go back in there. I ran to the neighbors' house but couldn't bring myself to say anything when the old lady next door answered. I was uncontrollable and delirious. I pointed next door and shouted, "Kate," in her face. She ran off to get her phone.

I sat on my front porch for what felt like hours. My mother told me later it was only seven minutes before the ambulance and police officers showed up, but I could have sworn I was sitting there for hours. I didn't say a word when they got there. They tried to get me to talk, but I just sat there shaking. The shaking wouldn't stop.

Kate, please wake up. They're trying to save your life in there right now. They're trying to wake you up. I can hear them trying to get you to take a breath, and you're refusing to do it. You want to go, but you have to stay. You have to stay. It isn't time for you to go yet. I can't do this without you, Kate, please just wake up. Please, Kate, please.

At some point, someone put a blanket around me that scratched my neck. Later on, my boyfriend and Jovie both appeared next to me. They tried to get me to go inside. I just sat there. My mother wanted to take the cootie catcher from my hand, but I screamed at her when she tried. I couldn't remember much over the past few hours, but I remembered that. I couldn't let go of it.

The sun went down and darkness engulfed the house, but I still just sat there. Once the police officers left, and Kate was pulled out of the house in a body bag, I finally got up. I moved to the porch swing and laid down. It was cold out, but I didn't feel much anymore.

Her body had been so warm. Her face had looked the same. Her face looked exactly the same. Why didn't she wake up? Why didn't she just wake up?

I moved the cootie catcher around in my hand and put my fingers in to play it. *Pick a number,* Kate would always say while she laughed. When it was her turn to play, she always picked thirteen. She said everyone always thought it was unlucky, so she felt sorry for it. I moved it back and forth until I got to thirteen. When I lifted the little flap on the side, it just said OPEN ME in Kate's bold handwriting.

I could feel my heart about to explode out of my chest as I slowly unwrapped her careful folding. The paper was creased and worn from my sweaty hands clutching it all evening. But I could still see her bright handwriting across it. The words were small, and, in the dim porch light, I had to squint to make out everything she had written. She had written in pencil, but it looked like she had written fast. She knew she didn't have much time.

Haddie,

All This Time in the Dark

I hope you find this before you come looking for me. Please don't look for me. Just call 911 and go wait on the porch. Remember how you used to sit on the porch swing for hours, and you would say it took all your cares away? Just sit there and wait. You were so dramatic back then. I always thought you would be an actress. Maybe you still can be.

I don't have anything to say to anyone except you, and all I keep thinking is how sorry I am. I'm sorry I got in Ian's car so long ago. I'm sorry I trusted him when you told me not to. I'm sorry I left you the night you were sick. I wish I would have stayed. I'm sorry I'm leaving you now, again. I don't want to go. I'm scared, and my hands are shaking. Maybe I feel like I don't have a choice. Maybe I'm just scared all the time. But, maybe, it's just so damn loud now. You know how that is? When the whole world around you is quiet because they're afraid of breaking you, but your mind is just so damn loud. It's just so, painfully, loud. When I close my eyes, I see those men over me. When I lay in bed, if I don't hold tight to my mattress, I feel like I might just float away into their arms again. Or back into that room again.

They won't remember me as "the survivor" anymore. That's what everyone calls me now, you know? "The Survivor." Like I did something worth remembering. Remember when we all used to watch Survivor *together at night? I feel like everyone thinks I won that show, but I didn't. They won't remember me like that now. They'll call me selfish. They'll all say I should have just gotten help, and I would have been okay. They'll call me a coward and say I took the easy way out. I know they will.*

And isn't that the problem? I might be taking the easy way out, but, dear God, I've already taken the hard way through. There were times over the past two years where I swore if I survived, I would come home, and everything would be okay. But now I'm home, and everything is so wrong. Everything hurts, and I don't remember home being so painful. Maybe I survived and came home, but I'm also not alive anymore and I know that. I'm not living. I'm just surviving, and that's no way to live.

I hope you don't think I'm selfish, sis. I can't control that, though. That's what they all say. "I can't control the cards I was dealt, but I have to deal with them now." Isn't that crass? I'm not strong enough to deal with this. I can't do it. I'm afraid of what it will look like on the other side of this. I'm afraid of who I'll become. That's what they won't understand when they say I'm so selfish. I'm really just a scared little girl inside. It's like I'm five, and it's dark, and I woke up from a bad dream, and all I want is my mommy to come into my room and hold my hand, and I'm screaming and screaming and getting more scared and nobody comes. Nobody is there.

Mom is going to be devastated. I know that. You are, too. And, in his own weird way, so is Dad. I get it. I'm sorry. I'm so, so, so sorry. But I'm so scared here in the dark. I'm so scared, and I want someone to come hold my hand. Right now, I want someone to come hold my hand because I don't want to go alone. I don't want to do this without my mommy and my sister. I don't. But I don't know what else to do, and I'm so scared. A part of me is hoping you'll burst through the

All This Time in the Dark

door and rush in and hold my hand and tell me it will all be okay. But I know it won't anymore.

I'm tired of being scared and alone in the dark, sis. I'm so sorry for being selfish. But I'm so scared here, and I just want to not feel scared anymore.

I love you, you know that? I'll be thinking of you and Mom and Jovie as I go. You'll bring me comfort in the dark. You'll always bring me comfort in the dark. If you're reading this, please know I'm not screaming from the nightmare anymore. The nightmare is over now, and I'm finally safe.

Love,
Kate

I folded the cootie catcher back along Kate's carefully folded lines. I swung my legs over the porch swing and sat up. Kate felt like she was alone in the dark for too long. I couldn't help her. I shouldn't have left her alone, and maybe I would feel guilty for that like I felt guilty for letting her meet Ian alone.

Kate was alone in the dark and we all left her there because we were all too selfish. We think about ourselves before anyone else. How many times do we walk by someone and say, "Hey, how are you?" and never even listen to the answer? Maybe that was the problem. Nobody wanted to hear her answers. We only hear what we wanted to hear.

Or maybe none of us were listening at all.

Kate was alone in the dark, and now I was, too. People like Ian and Mike were only too eager to creep in and steal someone's life away from them. When I was a kid, I used to think I could figure out world peace, and I didn't understand why that wasn't a thing. But now I knew why. Because men like Mike and Ian walk around in the world and think they know better and that some lives are worth more than others.

Tessa M. Osborne

I was alone in the dark now, but I didn't have to be. I finally stood up from the porch swing. My hands and feet were numb from the cold and from not moving for so long. I walked inside the house and found my Mom crying on the couch. I walked over to her and sat down.

"Mommy?"

She wrapped her arms around me. "Haddie, are you okay?"

"No, I'm not."

"I'm not either."

We sat on the couch the entire night together. I didn't know what we were going to do tomorrow or the next day. I didn't know how we would move past this. But I knew I couldn't be alone in the dark. I had to chase the light.

Ten Years Later

Haddie

The prison where Mike is held now is forty-five minutes away from my house. Every month, for the last three years, I drive those forty-five minutes telling myself I'm going to visit him. Just to talk to him. Just to see what he's really like. The news covered his story so many times, I lost interest in him for so long. But, over the last few years, so much changed. I wanted to see the man who stole my sister from me. Every month I drive forty-five minutes one way just to look him in the eye, and I can never even bring myself to make it inside. I always end up just driving back home.

Eric is perched on the edge of our bed, his dark blue jeans looking almost black against the pale white hands clasped in front of him. "Are you sure you don't need me to come with you?" he asks. He always asks me that. Every month, for the last three years, he has asked me that. First, he asked as the concerned boyfriend. Then he wondered as the curious fiancée. Now, I think he only asks out of marital obligation. I want to take him with me, but I've always felt seeing Mike was something I should do on my own.

"It's okay, hon. Thanks, though."

"At least let me drive you. I'll stop and visit my parents while you... you know... do your thing."

I sigh, "Okay."

"I don't have to go if you don't want me to."

"It's okay, I said."

"You don't seem happy about it."

"I didn't say that."

"You're acting annoyed."

"I just need time to think while I drive, I guess."

"I don't have to go."

I paused and smiled, "I just might not be chatty in the car, okay?"

"Okay."

Things had been tense between us lately. He wanted kids, and I did not. We each thought the other would change their mind. But, as the years together moved forward, we were both still stuck in the same mindset we'd had in college when we met. He always wanted kids, and I always wanted to avoid having them.

The drive to the prison was quiet. I watched the empty desert roll by outside Reno. It was lonely out here. Maybe that's why the prison was so far out here, alone. Nobody would miss it. I didn't think about Kate that much anymore. She died when I was only seventeen years old. And now, as a grown woman with a law degree, I didn't think much of the sister I sometimes missed so much it hurt. But, on the days when I drove to see Mike, I replayed every inch of Kate in my mind. Those were the days I missed her so much.

Eric never wanted to marry a lawyer. He said it all the time. That he never pegged himself as a guy who would marry the "high-powered attorney." He said it as an apology for the finer things he was afforded. My $10,000 retainer was responsible for his lifestyle, and he knew it. He was an elementary school teacher and often complained about being underpaid. I couldn't

All This Time in the Dark

apologize for the job I had, or the amount of work I'd done to get here. But I also had to love Eric, and sometimes there was no balance with that.

I froze when he pulled the car into the parking spot outside the prison. *The drive went by too fast,* I realized. *I can't go in there.*

Eric wrapped my hand in his. "You don't have to go in there," he said.

I looked towards him, and his eyes were so full of concern, so full of love for me, that I remembered why we fell in love in the first place. I remembered everything about how we met and danced, kissed, and held each other so clearly. It was in those moments that I hoped we could make it past everything that seemed to work its way between us. "I know I don't. But maybe I have to."

"Is it because of Penny?"

"It's so much of everything."

"You miss her today?"

"It hurts every day, but some days hurt more than others."

"You've come so far for someone who used to be so far in the dark."

"I wish Kate could be here with me to see Mike. She deserved that, you know?"

"I'm sorry, sweetie. I really am. I wish I could fix this for you."

I stepped out of the car after kissing Eric goodbye. He promised he would drive back as soon as I texted him that I was done and coming back out. His parents only lived twenty minutes away. I knew he would be there when I needed him.

My high heels clicked on the pavement as I walked towards the door. *Why is the door so far away?* I thought. It was an extensive process just to get into the prison to see a man serving a life sentence (and then some). Supposedly, he was a model prisoner. At least, my family's lawyer always assured us he was locked away and serving time the best way he could. That same lawyer, now a colleague of mine, was also a cocky bastard who thought Mike didn't get enough time behind bars in the first place.

Tessa M. Osborne

I had worn the gray suit I always wore for courtroom days. It fit the right way and the pants were the perfect length. I thought, if I felt good, then maybe I would simply just start to feel good. But it wasn't working. As I moved through the security process, I felt less sure that what I was doing was going to bring me any sort of peace. I was a family lawyer. I specialized in high-profile custody battles. I had no business being in a jail with a criminal.

By the time I sat down to face Mike, I was exhausted. After all those years of driving back and forth, I couldn't believe I was finally inside. *It's for Penny, you know. And, maybe because of Ian, too.*

I looked up. Mike was seated across from me, his orange jumpsuit not as bright as I would have expected. It looked like it was dull from years of washing and faded from days of neglect.

"You one of the family members?" He said it gruffly and with an air of boredom. He was not at all surprised to find me here and even less surprised that I was another family member of a woman he had hurt.

"My name is Haddie Jones. My sister, Kate…"

"I remember Kate," he interrupted. It surprised me that he would have remembered her from so many years ago. *It has been ten years now — how does he still remember Kate?* My hands were sweating.

"You do?"

"I called her something else, though. Probably a flower or a food name. I called all the girls flowers or foods." I looked him in the eye and realized he was crying as he said it.

"I don't really care about that."

He shrugged. "None of you ever do."

"I didn't come here for forgiveness."

"Then why are you here?"

"I had to face the man who ruined my life."

"What did you say your name was?"

"Haddie Jones."

All This Time in the Dark

"I've seen commercials for you on TV. You're a lawyer, aren't you?"

"I am."

"So, I guess I didn't ruin your *whole* life, did I?"

I paused. I hadn't expected that. Of course, he didn't ruin my entire life. He changed it. I hadn't had a plan until Kate was found dead. I hadn't even kind of known what I wanted to do or who I wanted to be. And then I realized I needed to help people, to protect girls like Kate.

"I guess not," I finally admitted, "but you did ruin my parents' lives."

"They get divorced?"

"My dad is dead," I answered. "He drank himself to death."

"Liver failure?"

"Car accident. Drunk driving."

"I wasn't behind the wheel of the car, Miss Jones, I didn't kill your father."

"Losing Kate killed my father. Watching his wife slip so deeply into depression, he couldn't get her out killed my father. He drank away his problems because he couldn't talk about them."

A tear rolled down Mike's cheek. "I wish I could change what I did."

"You sure about that?"

"My brother is dead, too, Miss Jones. People seem to forget about that."

"I saw on Facebook that Ian died. They said he never knew what you were doing. That he didn't have any fault with the life you created. If that was true, then why did he kill himself last year?"

"He used to come see me here, you know? He used to spend every weekend making the drive to come see me. After college, he moved to Sacramento. He was always looking for a new place to put down his roots. But he never could get away from his mind enough. I covered for him. I had to. I said I was the one responsible for every single woman I found, but we all know that wasn't true. Ian helped me because I paid him. It haunted him every day,

Miss Jones. Every single day. He knew women had died at my hands. He knew lives had been lost. He knew what he had done. But I left him with no choice, I guess. I was supposed to take care of him. I let him down."

"He led Kate right to you."

"He didn't have a choice."

"There's always a choice."

"Not when your brother threatens to disown you if you don't do what he says."

"You're pretty honest for a man who is responsible for the lives of multiple women."

"I've been in prison for a long time, Miss Jones. I've had a long time to think."

I nodded in return.

"You wanna know why I remember Kate so well? I don't remember all the girls. There were over fifty women I traded or bought or sold. I'm sure if I thought about it, I could remember all of them, but I don't. I don't think about it. Because that's a road that's too dark for even me to drive down. I can't do it. But some of them stand out — some of the ones who made a difference, like Kate. Ian didn't want to bring her to me. I made him. I knew she would be worth something, and he knew it, too. At first, he wanted to get close to her for me. But I saw something change in him when he was with her."

"Please don't tell me Ian loved her. I won't buy it."

"Suit yourself, Miss Jones, but the truth is what it is. He loved that girl. The night he brought her to me, we fought the entire time. I forced him to give me his phone. I arranged for him to pick her up. He was sick the entire night. She was the only girl he ever loved like that."

"I still don't believe you."

"It doesn't matter now, I guess. He spent nine years in hell over the things he did. A part of me is glad he doesn't have to do that to himself anymore."

All This Time in the Dark

I took a deep breath and looked away, "I'm not here to discuss Ian."

"I didn't think you were. I just thought you should know why he died."

"Because he felt bad?"

"Because he hated himself for what he did to your sister."

I nodded, "I see."

"So, what *did* you come here for?"

"I just needed to see your face."

"To tell me I ruined your life?"

"Well, I mean, yeah. But, also no, I guess."

Mike smiled. When he smiled, he looked like a normal, regular person. I didn't know how we had managed to hold a conversation like two people who weren't sitting in a prison, but we did. And I knew then how it was so easy for men and women to trust him. I would have trusted him if I had known better. I would have trusted him if his orange jumpsuit didn't slightly reflect the light above him, enough for me to keep some perspective.

"Miss Jones, I think we both know you came here out of curiosity. To find closure to this part of your life."

How did he know that I needed closure?

"Here's the thing, though," he continued, "you won't find that with me. I've had enough of you family members seek me out for revenge or hate or understanding. It's never about me. It's always about *you*. You all think that by sitting there and telling me I ruined your life, you'll feel better and happier, and like the world will be okay again. But it won't. Because no amount of acceptance here will bring your sister back. It just won't. I'm sorry for what I did ten years ago, Miss Jones. I hope you believe me when I say that. I am sorry for what I did. I found a way to make money when I was young, and I should have made better choices, but greed drives us to do stupid things. It drove me to lie and steal and cheat to get through life. It drove me to lose my brother, the one person I was supposed to protect forever, because of my selfishness. Your sister killed herself, didn't she? That's what they said in court, anyways, that she killed herself. But my brother killed himself, too. So, aren't we all just humans trying to make it through life?"

I didn't have anything to say. I didn't know what I was looking for from Mike anymore. I didn't know what closure I needed or what I had wanted to hear about Ian. I didn't even know if Mike was sincere. When I looked at him, he just looked so exhausted, like life had been too hard on him.

"I guess that's all I needed from you, sir. I should probably be going."

As I turned to get up, he called for me, "Miss Jones?"

I didn't sit back down. I held my coat between my hands so he wouldn't see my hands shaking. "What?"

"Kate was pregnant, wasn't she? I remember her so well. The way she looked when I asked her if she was pregnant. The way she looked so scared. I almost gave up right then. I almost stopped everything right then."

"Kate *was* pregnant. She had a girl. Her name is Penny. She was put up for adoption, but a few years ago, her family found me and my mother. Penny wanted to know where she came from. She's the most perfect little girl you could ever meet."

"Well, I'm glad we had a happy ending there, then."

"Do you know who the father was?"

"I wish I did, Miss Jones, but there were so many men that went through there. Your guess is as good as anyone else's."

I nodded. "Thank you for your time."

Mike half smiled. "All I have is time."

"One more thing," I said.

"Anything, Miss Jones."

"How did the cops find you? I was always told they had been tracing you for a while, and they finally found where you were. I couldn't find much more information on it than that."

Mike started to laugh. "Ian told them. He had left town to get as far away from me as he could. He couldn't forgive himself for Kate, though. One of the men who worked for me was a friend of Ian's. He told Ian that Kate was pregnant, so Ian called the police and told them where to find me."

Tears came to my eyes. "I didn't know that."

"There are always so many things people don't know about other people. Nobody asks anymore. We're all just kind of existing in this selfish place of thinking about how we can make it from one day to the next. It never occurs to us that everyone else is suffering through the same thing."

"I guess not."

"Thanks for coming by, Miss Jones."

"Thanks for seeing me."

"Go live your life. Don't let me ruin it any more than it already has been."

"It's not ruined, sir. I've never once lived my life alone in the dark like Kate had to."

"Thank God for that."

"No, sir, I thank myself for that. I worked hard to get where I am today."

"Good luck to you, then."

I walked out of the prison and did feel lighter. I didn't feel the weight of the world lift off my shoulders like I thought it would, but the day seemed a little easier now. It seemed easier to face a world without Kate in it. As I walked out of the prison, the sun was shining down on my face. I smelled the autumn air. I reached for my phone and texted the man I knew truly loved me, even though most days we hated each other.

I missed Kate. I missed my Dad. I wished I could pull my Mom out of the dark hole she had fallen into, but I couldn't. The assisted living facility she was in made sure she was okay, and I guess that was enough. I had the rest of my life ahead of me, and I couldn't let Ian or Mike ruin it any more than they already had. I was ready to move on. I was ready to live.

Acknowledgements

A huge thank you to Kelvin, my cover designer. Your encouragement and faith in me were much needed in a time when I wasn't sure I could do this. And a big thank you to Kasandra who found every flaw and made sure this would be my best writing. I appreciate your dedication to detail. Finally, to Remi, for answering my messages at one in the morning when I had no idea what I was doing. Thank you.

To my teachers in school who believed in me growing up, I don't think you have ever gotten the credit you deserved in life. Even if you don't remember me from way back when, I have always remembered your faith in me. Mrs. Hornberger, Mrs. Eck, Mr. Verdi, Mr. Lorentzen, and my college professors at SNHU. You all changed my life in wonderful ways. Never underestimate the difference you make in a student's life.

A thank you to my family and friends who consistently put up with me, especially: Dad, Gramma, Kimmie, Terry, Sunny, Trevor, Brooklyn, Mark, Maureen, Kathy, Nathan, Shawnice, Tricia, Kayla, Cindee, Jenna S., and all of my students, friends, and family who believe in me. I love you all, very much.

Tessa M. Osborne

A huge thank you to my sister. The sisters in this book were written because I think about you, and the way we grew up together, every single day. I will always love you.

The biggest thank you to my best friend, Cat. You support me, cheer me on, make me laugh, and always have my back. When I'm with you, it feels like a breath of fresh air. I love you, my sweet friend.

A gigantic thank you to my mother. When I was a little girl, you used to say you were always on my side. You've always kept your word, and, for that, I am more thankful than you will ever know. I look forward to seeing you and talking to you every day. I will always be thankful for everything you have done and continue to do for me. I love you, always.

The biggest thank you I have goes to my husband, Joshua. I used to hope I would find someone who loved me the way you do. I love you with everything I have.

And, finally, to Ben and Jack. You drive your mother crazy 98% of the time, but I love you both more than I ever thought possible. You are truly the best accomplishments in my life.

PS — Luckily, I've changed a lot since I was in high school. If I ever hurt you back then, I am so sorry. I am not the same person I was back then. Thank God for that. But, if you were ever mean to me, or didn't think I would amount to anything, you were wrong. And I will continue to prove that to you every single day.

www.ingramcontent.com/pod-product-compliance
Lightning Source LLC
Chambersburg PA
CBHW011141290426
44108CB00023B/2712